Life

After

Work

Life
After
Work

SIX RETIREMENT STORIES
THAT CAN CHANGE YOUR LIFE

Arthur F. Dauria, Ph.D.
and
Walter vom Saal, Ph.D.

Montrose Publishing, Montrose, PA

Life After Work: Six Retirement Stories That Can Change Your Life

Arthur F. Dauria, Ph.D. and Walter vom Saal, Ph.D.

Copyright 2007

ISBN 13: 978-0-9790775-0-0
ISBN 10: 0-9790775-0-8

First paperback printing July 2007

Front Cover image from photo © Tatiana Grozetskaya/www.fotolia.com

Printed in U.S.A.

Acknowledgements

We would like to thank Linda Condon, Cathy Harris, Kimberly Myers, Courtney Richards, and Jennifer Rokicki who provided research assistance for early drafts of this book. We would also like to thank Barbara Hein who provided us with excellent editorial help and some research assistance in the later stages of this book's production. Touchstone Communications provided valuable technical support and guidance throughout all the production and printing aspects of this book.

Many thanks to all the participants in our focus groups, workshops, and seminars; to the people who allowed us to interview them; and to the many individuals with whom we had informal discussions about retirement and life satisfaction. Their thoughts and experiences have helped us develop deeper insights and broader understandings of the issues that surround retirement.

Arthur Dauria would like to express his deep appreciation to his wife Barbara for being so supportive during the creation of this book, and in fact, for her support in all the dimensions of his professional life. He would also like to thank his children, Susan and Jodie for their support and understanding, and for the time this project took away from weekends that we might have spent together.

Walter vom Saal is deeply grateful to his partner Suzanne Miller for her loving support throughout the writing of this book. To his three children, Dan, Laura, and Jeff, he is very appreciative of their continued encouragement and willingness to help him think through his own feelings about the process of retirement. He also thanks Marshall and Dorian for their helpful insights.

The authors wish to dedicate this book to Walter's mother, Jane vom Saal, who finally has an answer to the question she started asking when Walter started teaching 30 years ago: "When are you going to write a book?"

Table of Contents

LIFE AFTER WORK

1

The Promise of Retirement

How and when will you retire? When you do retire, will you enjoy it? Is there anything you can do now to make your planned retirement more successful?

Millions of Americans are asking themselves these questions. There are 24 million people in the United States between the ages of 55 and 65. Most of them have either recently retired or are considering retiring in the not too distant future. For some of them, retirement will be a long anticipated transition to a new stage of life they look forward to with enthusiasm. For others it will be a change filled with anxiety, viewed as a loss, and leaving a void. For most, it will be an event filled with many mixed feelings—both losses and new opportunities. Retirement is both a sunset and a sunrise.

A person's life can be understood as a series of stages and transitions. The transition to retirement is different than it has ever been before. No longer is it just an ending and a move to a final stage of life. With people living longer and remaining healthier than ever before, today retirement can be viewed as a true beginning. It is a transition to a "second half" of adult life that can be long and satisfying. This makes it even more important to plan it well. Retirement has the potential to be a very positive transition or a very negative one. It can be a period with far more losses than gains, but it also can be a threshold to a new and extremely rewarding stage of one's life.

The purpose of this book is to offer some insights into the opportunities and pitfalls surrounding retirement. By examining some retirements that were successful as well as some that were not, we can learn more about how retirement can become a positive transition to an exciting new stage of life.

We became personally interested in retirement as we observed very different reactions to it in those around us. One man we knew had a long and satisfying career as a teacher, and was well loved by his students and respected in the small community where he lived. His wife also worked, and his family was warm and supportive. After more than a quarter of a century of teaching he chose to take advantage of an early retirement incentive program. Six months later, miserable and despondent over the loss of a career that had meant so much to him, he rigged a vacuum cleaner hose from his car's exhaust to its interior, sat in the car with the doors and windows closed, turned on the engine, and took his own life.

In the same town at about the same time, another person we knew also retired from teaching. His career also had been long and satisfying, and he also took advantage of an early retirement incentive program. In retirement he served in local government, and he converted his passion for collecting old and rare books into a small hobby/business run out of his home that provides some extra income. His friends describe him as active, energetic, involved, and even happier now than he was when he was working.

We wondered what makes one person's retirement a failure and another person's a success. Is it income? Is it planning? Is it health? Is it something in the person's character? Is it some level of self-understanding or self-awareness? Is it some combination of these things? Or is it something else entirely?

We explored these questions through interviews with retirees and those approaching retirement, and also through workshops, seminars, and focus groups that we conducted. We reviewed many books and articles written about retirement. We also looked for stories about people who retired—some who retired successfully and others less successfully. We found some fascinating stories that raise important questions about what is necessary for a rewarding retirement. They also offer powerful examples and instructive narratives that can help all of us think about how to make our own retirement productive and satisfying.

This book tells some of those stories—life stories that raise important questions about retirement, and suggest some answers.

LIFE AFTER WORK

Strategy of This Book

The approach taken in this book is different from the many other books about retirement on the market today. The vast majority of existing books on retirement relate to financial planning. While this is important, it is equally important to think about what we call the "personal side of retirement." As we will describe in much more detail later, financial security is not the only important issue in retirement. Beyond a certain level, more money does not lead to more happiness. Among the limited number of books that address issues beyond financial planning, some are self help books with advice about enjoying retirement. Others, such as Joel Savishinsky's *Breaking the Watch*,[1] report research and case studies of several people as they move through the transition of retirement. This book offers a different approach. It addresses retirement by telling the stories of several well-known people and their journey into the retirement phase of their lives.

The people we chose to profile are some of the most interesting and well-liked figures of our times. They are people many of us already know something about. All were significant personalities in their respective fields. They all achieved some measure of reputation or public importance. Most importantly, these are fascinating people who have had interesting lives. Their retirement stories are less well known, but have much to tell us. Reading about these people provides an enjoyable way to engage some of the critical issues about retirement and aging.

The people chosen for this book weren't chosen simply because their stories are interesting. Each of them offers insight into a particular theme that is important to retirement. They each represent an archetype of a central issue that many of us will face. Beyond that, their stories also offer opportunities to reflect on a broad set of questions about the factors that lead to a satisfying retirement.

Although these stories are about famous people, we believe they generalize to those of us with ordinary lives. While each of these stories is unique, each story also has some general themes that can be applied to all of us. These themes have common threads of importance regardless of fame, money, or social status.

People today are living longer and better now than ever before. Our search for an example of someone who lived a long and interesting life brought us to the Delany sisters. These two women each lived past the age of 100 years, and led productive and happy lives to the end. Their story is a compelling narrative of how age and longevity factor into the changing face of retirement. It reflects the hope so many of us hold about the possibility of living longer and more useful lives than those of generations past.

We wanted a profile of someone who had reputation and extensive wealth to see what might be learned about the role of money in the experience of retirement. This was especially significant since almost all the information available on the subject of retirement is financial information. Is it true that more money makes for a better retirement? The ads for financial planning would have us think that money is the key issue in retirement. And yet most of us know that for the people we see in our personal lives, money, beyond a certain level, has little correlation with happiness. We all know some people with relatively little money who are happy and others with plenty of money who are much less happy. Our search led us to Lee Iacocca. Mr. Iacocca was one of the wealthiest corporate leaders of his generation. What would his story of retirement tell us?

The central issues surrounding retirement can be very different for men and women. In exploring those differences we were also were led to confront several other issues. Many life styles and careers, often held by women, do not have a clear transition to retirement. When does one stop being a parent? When must a writer, or artist, or actor leave their profession? When does one stop working the farm? For women the kinds of work and tasks they dedicate their lives to are often more diverse and less organizational than the uni-dimensional strands that men typically choose. Relationships also seem to play a different role in the lives of women. Women are more likely to retire based on some relationship consideration. Our search for a story that incorporated several of these issues led us to Katharine Hepburn. She was one of the greatest actresses of the previous century but also had a complex and stormy relationship with another actor of equally notable fame—the self destructive and outrageous Spencer Tracy. The full depth of their personal relationship was little known in its own time. Only in the reflective biographies of Hepburn, and her autobiographies after Tracy's death, did we learn the true nature of this unconventional relationship. Hepburn's story illuminates some of the ways the retirement decision is often different for women. It is a story that speaks to the complexity of this issue as it relates to women, even women with some degree of fame, fortune, and unconventional careers.

Our search for a story about someone who entered retirement unprepared, unplanned, and lacking the resources once acquired in a successful life led us to Jimmy Carter. Most people know Carter only as the most respected ex-president and perhaps the most admired senior citizen in America today. He is the person most often identified as a role model of productive retirement. Few know how heartbreakingly difficult his path into successful retirement was, how long it took to reorganize his life after the failed attempt for a second presidential term, or the difficulties that were evolutionary steps in turning a most devastating failure into a productive later life.

And finally, health can be of central importance. We were interested in the role of health and general bodily decline as an issue in the retirement process. We were drawn to profiles of athletes, who, by necessity, are forced to end their careers earlier than most. Our search for someone who represented the struggle against bodily decline led us to the great tennis champion, Arthur Ashe. His life is an example of a person who also had to cope with another important factor—luck. Sometimes life just deals us a terrible blow that from all external accounts seems unfair. Arthur Ashe was forced to terminate his career early and then to cope with enormous adversity. His story is instructive and enlightening.

While many people may feel familiar with the broad outlines of these stories, we have included interesting details that most people do not know. We also have focused these stories on what they have to tell us about retirement. We have drawn from several much more comprehensive biographies and autobiographies about these individuals and we urge interested readers to look at these works. They are described more fully in the section on "For Further Reading" at the end of this book.

These stories are presented with a focus on what each has to tell us about the issue of retirement. Each account illuminates something about the opportunities or limitations of the retirement experience. There is no reason the chapters need to be read in any sequential order. It would be entirely appropriate, from our point of view, to turn to your favorite personalities and read those first, or to begin with those stories that illuminate the retirement issues most important to you. We hope that your interest will be stimulated to draw you into reading all the profiles here.

Our intention is to be instructive about the issue of retirement, not simply to tell a story that may have been told more completely in other places. Each narrative is followed by a discussion of several critical issues surrounding retirement. Each chapter concludes with some provocative reflections about the retirement experience that flow out of the narrative. Our goal in these concluding sections is to provoke further thought about what we see as the central issues that are always a part of this experience.

LIFE AFTER WORK

2

The Delany Sisters:
Living Long

Living Longer

Americans are living longer today than ever before in history. The change has been dramatic. Life expectancy in the United States at the turn of the last century was 47 years. Today it is 78 years, with the average male expected to live 75 years and the average female expected to live 80 years. One hundred years ago the chances of a person living past age 65 were only four in ten. Today they are more than eight in ten. The number of older persons in the United States is growing dramatically. In 1900 there were about 3 million people aged 65 and older; in 2000 this number had grown to 35 million. The Census Bureau projects it will be over 70 million by the year 2030. These changes are going to continue to accelerate. According to a recent prediction, today there are about 75,000 Americans age 100 and up, and that figure will rise to some 800,000 by the year 2050.[1]

This statistical reality is supported by personal experience. While each of us probably has some first hand knowledge of someone who died young, we also know many people who lived fruitfully well into their eighties and nineties. Local papers increasingly carry stories of people celebrating their 100th birthday—a phenomenon virtually unheard of a century ago.

In addition to living longer, people seem to be living better. Medical advances, extensive programs to help those who are older, more and more services for the elderly, better travel options, and the political influence of groups like the AARP have turned the retirement years into a potentially exciting and significant time for many.

It is critical to understand that the image many have of the elderly is driven by unfortunate stereotypes and a youth-obsessed media industry. The majority of the elderly are healthy. Talking about someone who is advanced in age conjures up images of people in nursing homes, but this image does not match the true reality. In fact, only 1 in 20 older Americans is in a nursing home. The vast majority of those over age 65 are healthy and able to continue active, productive lives.

Consider what this means for retirement. For the growing number of individuals who live productively into their late eighties and beyond, their years in retirement may actually equal or be longer than their years of employment. In today's society, it's entirely possible for a person to start his or her productive career at age 25, and to consider retirement at age 55, with a productive working career of thirty years. Today the average 55 year old can expect to live more than another 25 years.[2] That means they can expect to spend almost as many years in retirement as they did in their entire working career. This is especially true of those whose careers started late, such as professional people who spend many years in an educational system, women who start a career after raising a family, or those who found their career of choice well into adulthood. It also will be true for the increasing number of people who retire even earlier than age 55.

This greatly extended life span has major implications for retirement. Retirement is increasingly being described as a mid-life transition into the "second half" of adult life. No longer is this period of life seen as the ending of useful life, a period of deterioration and decay. Instead, we now realize that for many fortunate individuals there will be a long period of energetic and productive living. Indeed some have described this as the most rewarding stage of life, a stage where the pressures of making a living and striving for success are no longer the dominant themes of our lives.

Perhaps no story illustrates this better than that of the Delany sisters: Sarah Louise ("Sadie") and Annie Elizabeth ("Bessie"). Born of a father who had been a slave in the south, the sisters went on to distinguished careers in education and dentistry. But even more remarkable than their careers was the length and productivity of their retirement. They were both over 100 years old when they wrote their first book, *Having Our Say,* which became a national best seller, and led to interviews, TV appearances and national visibility. Having become modern icons of aging well, the Delany sisters merit a closer look as hopeful examples of aging and retirement that are truly remarkable.

The Backstory

"When you get real old, honey," said Bessie Delany, "you lay it on the table. There is an old saying: Only little children and old folks tell the truth."[3] And what an extraordinary truth it was. At the age of 101 and 103 Bessie and Sadie Delany shared their life story and wisdom with Amy Hill Hearth, a reporter they first met when she came to interview them for a *New York Times* article. Their subsequent conversations resulted in a book that became a national best seller. ***Having Our Say: The Delany Sisters' First 100 Years***, raised the hopes and consciousness of thousands of readers about the prospect and possibility of living a quality life to the age of 100.

Their book was so popular that the Delanys wrote a second book, ***The Delany Sisters' Book of Everyday Wisdom***, at the ages of 103 and 105. The sisters achieved a certain level of fame, appearing on national TV shows and in numerous newspaper and magazine articles. A Tony-nominated Broadway play was written about their lives in 1995. And then finally, Sadie wrote ***On My Own at 107***—her book about life after Bessie's death.

The story of the Delany sisters is a story of two feisty, intelligent, accomplished, black women who both lived to see more than a century of productive life. Daughters of a father born into slavery and a mother who could have passed for white (but chose not to), these two women began life in the rural south and finished their days in cosmopolitan New York. Disciplined, hard working and intelligent, the sisters achieved quality educations, gained professional respectability, became pacesetters, and at the age of 100, worked their way into the hearts of millions.

People are increasingly living to older ages, and spending many more years in retirement than ever before. The most important consideration for them is: can this longer life be a life with quality? The Delany sisters are shining examples of lives lived long and well. Theirs is a remarkable story of personal achievement, longevity, and human charm.

The Family

If there is a compelling reason for the outstanding success of the ten Delany children, it has to be the dedication and values of the parents, Henry and Nanny Delany. Henry and Nanny were exceptional people. They were extremely intelligent, focused, shrewd, accomplished, and dedicated to their children. Henry started life as a slave child on a Georgia plantation and took advantage of every opportunity open to him. The time of his young life was a time of reconstruction and reorganization in the south. Many newly freed blacks found themselves actually worse off then they had been in slavery. Because they had been house servants, the Delanys suffered fewer privations than those slaves who typically worked their masters' fields. They also enjoyed the advantage of literacy, as their owner had encouraged his slaves to learn to read and write. Set free at the age of seven by the Emancipation Proclamation, Henry and his family left the plantation with nothing but the shirts on their backs. He worked hard as a mason and struggled to get an education. Henry's parents' marriage was recognized by their owners, and his immediate family had remained intact throughout their period of slavery. This may be the most important factor explaining the strong, nurturing family life and resilience in the face of difficulties that Sadie, Bessie and their siblings enjoyed.

After a jarring adjustment period, Henry, a Methodist, was befriended by a white Episcopalian Priest who determined to help him go to college. With that help, Henry was enrolled at St. Augustine's, a "School for Negroes" in Raleigh, North Carolina. This experience was a long way from the Georgia/Florida experience of his youth, both physically and psychologically. But Henry Delany was up to the challenge.

While attending St. Augustine's, Henry met and courted Nancy Logan, another student, who was the belle of the campus. She became the class valedictorian; he became the salutatorian. The two were married in the campus chapel in 1886.[4] Henry went on to have a teaching role in the same school and eventually become school's vice principal. In 1918 he became the first elected black bishop of the Episcopal Church.[5] By Sadie's account her father was a smart, good-looking man with reddish brown skin, who was exceptionally dedicated to his wife and family.

Nanny Logan was born in Virginia, in 1861 to an "issue-free Negro" mother who was herself only one-quarter black (her maternal grandfather had been a slave). Her father, James Miliam, was a white man who never married, but maintained a stormy, unconventional yet committed relationship with Nanny's mother, Martha Logan. Miliam built Martha a cabin near his own house with a wooden walkway between them so he could go back and forth without getting his boots muddy.

Nanny was considered "colored," and was proud of her black heritage. According to Sadie, she never tried to "pass" for a white woman.

Nanny Logan spent a sweet and carefree childhood in Yak, Virginia. She grew up in the supportive environment of a non-traditional but very caring family. So supportive in fact, that when the young Nanny set her sights on going to St. Augustine's School her mother packed her bags and went with her—and the entire time Nanny was a student there, her mother was nearby working odd jobs to support herself. The family was quite devoted to each other. James Miliam died in despondency soon after Martha's death, and left all his possessions and land to Nanny.

St. Augustine's School ushered in a new era of stability, challenge and order into Henry's and Nanny's lives. They met and flourished there. Once there they not only distinguished themselves academically, but they stayed on after graduation to thrive in its supportive environment. This was quite an accomplishment for blacks attempting to get an education in the post-reconstruction south. While there was general agreement that education was essential for personal advancement, most white universities were either inaccessible or inhospitable to black people. Women of this era were not expected to get an education, so their possibilities were even more limited. Black colleges flourished in this time but the number was far too few to accommodate the vast need. It was fortunate indeed that Henry and Nanny both came to rest at St. Augustine's, where they both distinguished themselves. He rose to the position of school administrator, and she worked as a matron, and they remained there for all of their working lives. The school gave them both the time and resources to devote to their large family.

It was there that they produced ten children "of every shade from white to brown sugar."[6] Sarah Louise, who was always called Sadie, was the second of ten children, born on September 19, 1889. Annie Elizabeth, born two years later, was known as Bessie. The two were inseparable. Sadie said:

> I came into this world at 7:30 in the evening on the nineteenth day of September, 1889. It was a day of hard labor for Mama. . . . Mama got her confidence back with my birth, and went on to have eight more healthy babies . . . Next in line was Annie Elizabeth, born two years after me and known as Bessie. I don't remember life without Bessie.[7]

Sadie and Bessie remained close throughout their long and productive lives. They were a complement to each other. Sadie was calm, organized and caring. The "smoother of waters." Bessie was feisty, outgoing, and hot tempered — "Queen Bess," as Henry used to call her.[8] Both women believed that Bessie possessed some dimension of intuitive power bordering on that of a "psychic."[9] While very different in nature, the sisters enjoyed each other, and each one valued the qualities that the other brought to their relationship.

The Delany children led a happy but sheltered existence, rarely venturing beyond the bounds of St. Augustine's School. The children were not permitted to go off the campus without an escort. The children enjoyed a happy, secure childhood, bathed in the loving guardianship and tutelage of their parents, and the educational direction of a gifted, devoted teaching staff. So powerful was this grounding, that when Sadie died in 1999, she left more than one million dollars to the school.

Leaving St. Augustine's

As each of the children matured and left the enlightened domain of the St. Augustine campus, they encountered the wider world of harshness of the "Jim Crow" south. The Supreme Court had formalized segregation through Plessy v. Ferguson, which legalized "separate but equal" public school facilities for white and nonwhite students. For Sadie and Bessie this outside world of segregation and racism was a sharp departure from the supportive experience of St. Augustine's. Both Sadie and Bessie got teaching jobs after graduation and began to understand and experience the second class status of being black in the south. "We knew we were second class citizens, but those Jim Crow laws set it in stone,"[10] said Sadie. In the heat of the legally segregated south, blacks felt the sting of separate—and inferior—amenities in every aspect of their lives. Schools, transportation, hospitals, restaurants—even restrooms and water fountains were segregated.

For Sadie and Bessie, after the nurturing experience of their youth, the central organizing theme of their adult lives was the challenge of overcoming the pain and humiliation created by discrimination. Their responses were based on the strong family values they received from their parents. There are many ways people in the Delanys position could respond to racism, but their father was very clear about what the response would be in the Delany family. Henry Delany maintained that the way to deal with racism was to just do your job better than anyone else around. All ten of the Delany children took that message to heart by pursuing higher education and careers as respected professionals.[11]

Rather than become bitter and angry, the Delany sisters adopted their parents' advice: work hard, excel, and keep to high moral standards. The family shared the belief that true equality would come only through excellent achievement. While this principle would guide the Delany sisters throughout their adult lives, in the culture of segregation, it was far from a smooth ride.

When Sadie graduated from the two-year program at St. Augustine's, her father urged her to go on to a four-year college, telling her, "you owe it to your nation, your race, and yourself to go."[12] Mr. Delany had little money, but he insisted that Sadie not take a scholarship, cautioning her that if she did so, she would be beholden to the people who gave her the money.

The sisters had been brought up believing that by getting ahead they could change the world a little, thereby helping their people. Bessie and Sadie would hold fast to this family belief throughout the duration of their professional and personal lives.

Both of the sisters made the decision to pursue careers. They had seen their mother raise ten children, and Sadie, in particular, was adamant that such a path was not what she wanted for herself. Both of them dated and had some serious relationships with men, but in those days marrying and having a family made it very difficult to have a career. Indeed, teachers often were forced to choose between marrying and following their profession. Eventually, both sisters chose a career instead of raising a family.

Both Sadie and Bessie took teaching positions in local schools. For both sisters, the teaching experience was their first time away from home alone. Both young women saved every penny so they could afford to continue their education.

During this period Sadie learned how to drive, and when Booker T. Washington came to visit Raleigh, she borrowed her brother Lemuel's car so that she could show the influential black educator some of the schools in her district. This was the first of many encounters the Delany sisters would have with influential black leaders throughout their lives.

The two sisters had different approaches to the sting of segregation and discrimination. Sadie, in keeping with her softer personality, would just "laugh it off." In her memoir, Sadie tells of how she would pretend ignorance of the demeaning Jim Crow laws while shopping for shoes in Raleigh. She didn't blame the store owner for the rule that prohibited her from sitting in the white section, she just ignored it. He was disarmed by her friendly, assertive demeanor, and was unable to confront her.

In this store, the white shoppers sat in the front to try on shoes, but the black shoppers had to go to the back. Sadie would go in and say to the shop owner: "Good morning, Mr. Heller, I would like to try on those shoes in the window."

He would say, "That's fine, Miss Delany, go on and sit in the back."

Then she would say, "Where, Mr. Heller?"

And he would gesture to the back and say, "Back there."

And she would say, "Back where?"

Finally, the owner would give up and say, "Just sit anywhere, Miss Delany!"

And then, Sadie reports in her memoir, "I would sit myself down in the white section, and smile."[13] In her calm and persistent manner, while not directly confronting the racism, Sadie got her way.

Bessie was different. She bridled more outwardly against the injustice and had many defiant brushes with established practices. She was the one who was likely to drink from the white fountain, to return an insult, to openly fight the injustice. It was Bessie who openly confronted a drunken white man who approached her in the colored waiting room of a train station in Waycross, Georgia.

The man began shouting over and over "the nigger bitch insulted me!"

A white crowd began to form. As the crowd grew, it turned into the kind of show-down that often resulted in blacks being lynched. Only the luck of her train arriving saved Bessie from such a fate. And even though she knew she was lucky to be alive after the confrontation she still claimed she "would rather die than back down."[14]

But even with all her spirit and feistiness, Bessie realized the self-destructive power of anger and bitterness and did her best to avoid it. "If you asked me how I endured it, I would have to say it was because I had a good upbringing. My parents did not encourage me to be bitter."[15]

While both sisters felt wounded by the injustice of segregation, and while they protested it in different ways, both maintained a balanced attitude toward social justice. They realized all white people were not of one mind. The Delany sisters determined to cultivate goodness in every corner of their lives. They refused to be consumed by resentment.

College

In 1915 the sisters had made their first trip to New York, traveling with their mother. Some time later, when somebody asked if they had seen the Statue of Liberty, one of the sisters replied, "Tell you the truth, we didn't care too much about it. The Statue of Liberty was important to white European immigrants. It was a symbol to them. We knew it wasn't meant for us."[16] What did impress them, however, was the action and excitement of Harlem. It made such an impression that both young women would soon move north.

In 1916, Sadie moved to New York City to attend college. Bessie arrived a year and a half later. Sadie enrolled in the domestic science division of the Pratt Institute. At that time, Pratt was only a two-year college. So after graduation she enrolled in Columbia University's Teacher College in order to acquire a four year teaching degree.

Bessie enrolled in a dental degree program at Columbia University in the fall of 1919. She was the only black woman in the entire class. The program was extremely challenging. The first two years of dental school, at that time, was identical to medical school. The dental class even had to dissect cadavers.

In dentistry school Bessie faced a continuous struggle to overcome prejudicial treatment. She had difficulty with some professors who did not like the fact that a black woman had been admitted to Columbia. While some professors treated her extremely well, she discovered that one professor graded her lower than white students, even for identical work. Recalling the Columbia experience, Bessie remarked, "I suppose I should be grateful to Columbia, that at that time they let in colored people. Well, I'm not. They let me in but they beat me down for being there!"[17]

She ran into prejudice even on her graduation day. Bessie was selected as a graduation marshal by her fellow students. She later overheard some students talking and discovered that she had been selected only so the other students would not have to march beside her in front of their parents.

The move to New York City, while not free of trials and prejudice of its own, placed the sisters in the center of an exciting experience known as the Harlem renaissance. There were writers like Langston Hughes and James Weldon Johnson, and jazz artists like "Jelly Roll" Morton, Louis Armstrong and Bessie Smith. There were hundreds of churches and an active religious and social life. While immersed in this new experience, the sisters did not lose their close family connections since nine of the Delany siblings eventually came to New York.

Young Professional Women

After graduating from Columbia in 1920, Sadie got her first job teaching at P.S. 119, an elementary school in Harlem. She would continue to work in the New York City school system throughout her career. She was hard working and enterprising, and no work seemed to be beneath her. She made extra money by baking cakes and selling them for a nickel a slice to other teachers at school. She also made lollipops and sold them in the school cafeteria for a penny apiece. A friend traveled around the city marketing her candies. Sadie continued making candies for many years, selling under the name "Delany's Delights."

Soon after Sadie started her teaching career, Bessie was ready to open up a dental practice. She shared an office in

Harlem with her brother Hap, who, although four years younger, had already graduated from dental school and begun his practice.

There were many dentists during Bessie's years of practice who would not accept any black patients, which is why, Bessie notes, it was essential that there were black dentists. On one occasion, a former white classmate from Columbia called Bessie to tell her that he was sending over a patient. Bessie thought that her classmate was doing her a favor until he mentioned that the patient happened to be his maid. Immediately Bessie realized that her classmate didn't want to work on this patient because she was black. She told him, "You are not a doctor of dentistry! You are a doctor of segregation!" yelling so loudly that he quickly hung up.

Bessie was willing to help any patient who came to her, no matter how sick or how destitute. When Bessie started her practice in 1923, she charged five dollars for a silver filling, and two dollars for a cleaning. When she retired in 1950, she was still charging the same rates.

Father's Death and the Depression Years

A significant change in the lives of the Delany sisters occurred when their father died in 1928 at the age of 70.[18] They got a telegram that he was gravely ill and they should come quickly, but by the time they arrived he had died. The children all decided that it would be best for their mother to move north to be closer to most of them. She would live with Sadie and Bessie. After almost half a century living at St. Augustine's, it must have been wrenching for her mother to make such a move and leave so much behind. Bessie remembered a touching scene of her mother, taking all the old love letters from her husband into the courtyard, reading them, and burning them one by one. The children didn't want her to do it but she insisted. It was an act of total separation from the past. This must have brought home to Sadie and Bessie the enormity of their new obligation to take care of their mother in the remaining years of her life.

Although they were both educated working women, life was hard for the Delany sisters during the depression, but once again, it was the family that held them together. Sadie was fortunate that she held a job in the New York City school system, so her income remained reliable throughout the depression. For Bessie it was a different story. Most of Bessie's patients couldn't pay her, and would often show up at her office not only needing medical attention, but also needing food, clothing, or other types of assistance. Bessie had a reputation for helping those in need. Once she gave a patient her only radio because she thought the patient, who lived alone and was very poor, would enjoy it more than she would.[19] A patient of hers once said, "Your office isn't a dentist's office. It's a social services agency!" With little money coming in, Bessie's income dropped, and she found herself evicted from her own office twice before the economic climate improved.

Throughout the depression years and beyond, the Delany family remained close. The nine brothers and sisters got together almost daily, usually meeting in the office shared by Bessie and her brother Hap.

It was during the depression that Sadie made a career move that she remained proud of all her life. She became the first African American teacher of domestic science in the New York City high schools.[20] The way it happened shows her pluck and courage. Her years teaching at the elementary level put her near the top of the list of candidates for transfer to high school level, which was considered a promotion because it paid more and carried more prestige. But she knew that when the white people who would interview her saw that she was black, they would find some way to pass over her. So she followed the advice of a friend and wrote them with an excuse that she couldn't make that interview, so they would not know her race. She was hired based on her credentials, then she just showed up on the first day of class when it was too late for them to do anything about it. Looking back, she laughed thinking about the looks on their faces when they saw her that day. But it wasn't easy, and she was shunned by most of the white teachers in the teacher's lunchroom. It showed courage, not only to buck the system in the first place, but to come to work day after day to a place where she knew most of her colleagues were negative and even hostile. Once again she carried out her father's advice about the best way to confront racism—just do your job, and do it as well or better than anyone else around you.

In 1945 Sadie, Bessie, and their mother moved to a small cottage in the Bronx. For many years after the move to New York, Mrs. Delany had enjoyed excellent health, and was able to visit Niagara Falls, attend the 1932 Olympics in Los Angeles, and even travel abroad with Sadie. But now she began to show signs of decline. She became forgetful and occasionally confused, and the two sisters began to worry that she would leave a stove on or do something else that was dangerous.

Retirement

A decision was made that someone needed to stay home to take care of their mother. Giving this task to someone outside the family seemed out of the question, and the possibility that it might have been one of the brothers or another sister seems never to have been considered. So either Bessie or Sadie would have to retire to care for their mother. The logical choice was Bessie, since Sadie's teaching job would produce a pension if she stayed on another ten years. Sadie's pension would be $150 per month. Not a lot of money, even back then, but as Sadie said to Bessie "That would be $50 for Mama, $50 for you, and $50 for me."[21] They thought they could get by on it if they were very careful with their money. Bessie, on the other hand, had no pension with her private dental practice. She was only 59 and hadn't planned to retire yet, but she accepted the family decision that she should be the one to retire and care for their mother.

Bessie had never been much of a housekeeper, but now she plunged into making their little cottage nicer than it had ever been. The doorknobs shined so much that someone once asked if they were made of gold. Looking back later, Bessie regretted that she had worked so hard keeping their little cottage perfect. It was only after her mother died and Bessie became old herself that she realized her mother didn't care so much that the cottage was perfect. Late in her life, Bessie would look back with regret at this missed opportunity: "… she didn't want brass fixtures that gleamed like gold, she wanted me."[22]

When their mother passed away calmly in her sleep at home in 1956, at the age of 95, it must have seemed like the end of an era. As the eldest sister, Sadie was now the "head of the

29

family," and she was consulted for all family decisions. This did not sit easily with Bessie, who was feisty and independent, but she accepted it as the way things were supposed to be.

Bessie took Mama's death hard, but it was even harder on Sadie. She "cried for weeks and weeks. Every time we sat down for a meal, with Mama's chair sitting there empty, tears would come streaming down Sadie's face."[23] Sadie described herself as a "Mama's child," and even after she moved to New York she wrote her mother at least one letter a day, sometimes two. After her mother died, Sadie said later, "I thought, Maybe I should die myself."[24] Sadie plunged into a period that she would later admit was depression. It was partly for this reason that Bessie urged a move to Mt. Vernon. Sadie said later:

> Bessie . . . had an ulterior motive in moving us out of the Bronx. She says she didn't think I would ever get over Mama's death, and that maybe by moving away and starting over, it would help. I think she was right.[25]

They purchased a two-family house on the same street in Mount Vernon where their brother Hap lived. They rented half of the building to their sister Laura and her husband. Hap had been the first black to move into the neighborhood a few years earlier. The way he made that move showed the typical Delany courage and persistence in the face of a hostile white world. When realtors consistently found reasons not to show him houses in white neighborhoods, he bought a piece of land and had a house built. Some of the neighbors were not pleased when they discovered that the family moving in was black. And when they moved there, the Delany sisters faced a similar reaction. A white woman from Welcome Wagon stopped by to welcome the new family, and assumed Bessie must be the new family's maid. The feisty Bessie exclaimed, "Lady I have news for you. I am the owner." [26]

The move was a good one. Their house was at the end of the street, and faced away from the other houses, with a view of New York City in the distance. The first thing they did was add a porch. Well acquainted with the commonly held belief that black residents brought down a neighborhood because they didn't keep up their property, the sisters soon had the most well-groomed yard on the block. Bessie and Sadie set out to create the best garden anyone could find, and they derived a great deal of pleasure from the pursuit. Their garden would remain a major focus of Bessie's life. She worked in it until over the age of 100. Indeed, it was at age 98 that her sister finally convinced her she should no longer climb the ladder each year to cut the branches that grew to block their view of the city. For many years, elderly residents from the nearby white retirement home would walk over to look at the large variety of flowers and vegetables that the sisters had planted.

Sadie retired from teaching in 1960, at the age of 70. The sisters remained active and energetic throughout their many years of retirement. One of their favorite activities was to have dinner guests. They even kept a book noting what was served to each guest, so that when they had someone back they would not serve the same thing.

Throughout their long retirement period they continued to live very frugally. They never bought soap in their lives, always making their own with a recipe that included lye and meat fat. They refused to own a telephone, claiming it was one of the great interferences of modern life. Their television set was one given to them in 1950, and they found it perfectly fine for them—especially since they preferred radio. When they moved into the Mt. Vernon house they bought their furniture from the Salvation Army and they were very happy with it. Both sisters seemed committed to a basic, healthy, non-consumer oriented lifestyle. Their basic values revolved around family, love, kindness, discipline, and responsibility. Material things were never important to them. They often turned away from material gain in favor of family or kindness.

They also continued to follow the family motto of helping others. They were particularly proud of having saved the life of their young cousin Daisy from the south. They heard that she was dying of pellagra and the doctor said that nothing could be done. Sadie, who was aware of developments in nutrition, took pains to find out the most recent discoveries and found that the disease was due to a vitamin B deficiency. She sent Daisy some vitamins that could only be bought in New York along with a schedule for taking them and a set of diet plans—which eventually saved Daisy's life. They continued to send her vitamins and extra money for her expenses every month until she died many years later in her eighties.[27]

They had a daily routine that they were convinced added to their longevity. Sadie and Bessie would usually rise at 6:30 a.m., and start the day with a session of yoga. Sadie was the leader in this activity, and sometimes she would look around and find that Bessie was "cheating," lying on the floor instead of doing her yoga, and she urged Bessie to continue. Their exercise program was followed by a full glass of water, a teaspoon of cod liver oil, and a raw clove of garlic swallowed whole. When Bessie and Sadie moved to Mt. Vernon, they continued to boil the tap water that they used for drinking. They were constantly being told that this was an unnecessary precaution, since the city of Mt. Vernon purified its water supply. The sisters, however, had been drinking boiled tap water since they were children, and weren't about to relinquish a life-long habit.[28]

After exercising, the sisters would prepare breakfast. It was the largest and most important meal of the day, consisting of a scrambled egg, a hard roll, a piece of fruit, and a bowl of oatmeal. Bessie and Sadie rarely had to buy vegetables because their garden was so productive. They made a point of eating seven different vegetables every day, many from their own garden. One way to do this was to prepare dishes in which they were able to use all of their vegetables at once.

At midday, the sisters would have a large, well-balanced meal. In keeping with their Southern tradition, they called their mid day meal "dinner." It usually consisted of either chicken or beef accompanied by an extensive variety of homegrown vegetables.

Whereas breakfast was usually followed by morning prayers and a quiet time for reading, the afternoon ushered in an important daily event—the arrival of the mail. Since Sadie and Bessie had no desire to get a telephone, the mail served as a vital link with the outside world. The remainder of the afternoon was usually spent answering correspondence, paying bills, and taking a short walk.

The sisters would always have a light evening meal, usually a vanilla milkshake, after which they would head upstairs to watch the *MacNeil/Lehrer News Hour.* Says Amy Hill Hearth, co-author of the three Delany sisters books, "The sisters, in fact, are the most well-informed people I know, which is one reason it is sometimes hard to remember that they are more than 100 years old."[29]   Sadie and Bessie's day would always close with an evening prayer session, after which Sadie would turn in for the night, and Bessie would tune in to talk radio.

When Amy Hill Hearth interviewed them in 1991 for an article in the *New York Times*, Bessie had just celebrated her 100th birthday and Sadie her 102nd.   Hearth described them as truly remarkable. She found them to be energetic, active, and involved in their daily life. The sisters still had a love and passion for life, enjoyed living, and felt useful and positive even at this advanced age.

The *New York Times* article started a productive relationship between Hearth and the Delany sisters that resulted in three books about the lives of the Delany sisters. The article led to wide interest in these impressive centenarians, and Amy Hill Hearth worked with them for the next two years to co-write their book, *Having Our Say: The Delany Sisters' First 100 Years.* It was published in 1993, and stayed on the *New York Times* best-seller list for over two years. Another book, The *Delany Sisters' Book of Everyday Wisdom,* followed in 1994. Their story was turned into a Broadway play, and there were appearances on several TV shows including the *Oprah Winfrey Show.* Throughout all this popularity and attention, the sisters retained their simple down to earth lifestyle and personal view of what was really important in the world.

The final major transition of Sadie's life occurred on September 25, 1995, when Bessie passed away peacefully at home at the age of 104. Many thought that Sadie, having lost her lifelong companion and her only remaining sibling, would have little left to live for and would soon follow her sister. Indeed, Sadie herself thought that might be what would happen, but later she was to say "it just wasn't my time." When an interviewer asked Sadie what she would do now that Bessie had died, Sadie replied "another book!"[30] At the age of 107 she was certainly not ready to stop living.

Amy Hill Hearth, who would work with her on this book, said that:

> . . . creating this book would give new meaning to Sadie's life, providing a mechanism for her to express her feelings as well as fulfilling her ongoing need to be useful and productive. . . . [The book became] the story of one woman's evolution, over the course of a year, from despair to hope. Sadie Delany has given us an invaluable gift: She shows us that even at the age of 107 it is possible to begin again.[31]

When Sadie died peacefully in her sleep at the age of 109 it marked the end of a remarkably long and interesting life.

In his book *Defy Aging*, psychologist Michael Brickey described the ingredients necessary for leading a fuller, more rewarding life now that people are living longer and enjoying better health. According to Brickey:

> You need a vision of healthy aging focused on what is possible rather than what has been. You need a continually renewing sense of purpose all your life. You need attitudes, beliefs and a lifestyle that foster health and longevity. And you need to defy conventional thinking about aging.[32]

It should come as no surprise that Brickey chose to illustrate these traits by telling his reading audience a little about the Delany sisters—Sadie and Bessie.

LIFE AFTER WORK

What the Delany Sisters' Story Tells Us

The Delany sisters are unique in many ways. The rest of us are not very likely to live to 109, or write a best selling book at 102. But the Delany story is an inspiring one and it offers many guidelines for successful retirement that can be instructive to all of us.

Retirement May Last a Very Long Time

The most striking message from the lives of the Delany sisters is that the retirement years, which were once considered an afterthought following a lifetime of work, may themselves be an extended period of valuable time. While the Delany sisters lived longer than most of us will live, they illustrate a powerful trend. As was pointed out in the chapter introduction, the statistics tell us that life expectancy has grown dramatically over the last century, and will continue to grow.

The Delany sisters also show us that this long period can be one of active and productive living. Not only did they live to the ages of 104 and 109 years, but they remained active, energetic, alert, and healthy. They lived lives that were positive, optimistic, and cheerful until the end. The statistics tell us that people are not only living many more years, but that for most of those years they will be active and healthy.

These changes have profound implications for retirement. While retirement was once considered the final life transition just prior to decrepitude and death, it is increasingly becoming a late mid-life transition into a long period of useful and interesting living. Retirement is no longer something that happens at the tail end of life, when productivity is declining, energy is low, and the end is near. It is often an extended period of happy productive living, where people find the time and ability to address significant issues like family, friendships, travel, hobbies, or even immersion into a second vocational interest. It can be an exciting period of life where the pressures of success are replaced by the pleasure of pursuing significance. And while we are not suggesting that this prediction will come true for everyone, it certainly will come true for greater numbers of people than ever before in our history.

The central message for all of us is that retirement should no longer be considered just an ending. As we contemplate our retirement, we should plan for a new stage of life that can be long, productive, and satisfying.

Relationships Are Important

For Sadie and Bessie, as for most of us, relationships played a central role in their retirement as well as throughout their lives. No one could read the Delany sisters' books without coming to the conclusion that the most important thing in their lives was their relationship with each other. Each was a friend, supporter, helper, companion and soul-mate to the other. Sadie and Bessie lived together for over 100 years. They were the most important people in each other's lives. Sadie, describing the joy in her life said: "my joy is Bessie."[33] They were best friends and life partners, in some ways playing the role that a spouse might play in a married person's life. When Bessie died, Sadie said she was not sure she could go on without her.

After their relationship with each other, the relationships that were most important to the Delany sisters were their family. The family was profoundly important for all the Delanys.

Beginning at St. Augustine's in Raleigh, and continuing as most of the children moved north to New York City to pursue their careers, the family provided stability and support throughout their lives. The Delany sisters continued to see their brothers and sisters almost every day; they wrote daily to their mother. All of the family members provided comfort and support to each other in times of crisis and change.

For the Delany sisters their most significant relationships were with each other and their close family. For others of us, the most significant relationships might be with spouses or partners, or children, or extended family, or a few close friendships, or broader social networks in church or community. But whatever the pattern, most people do have a complex network of relationships, with a few core relationships that are central and crucial.

Relationships need to be taken into account in retirement. People age and retire better when their relationships are healthy. Research on happiness shows that for many individuals the primary determinant of their happiness is the quality of their relationships. This can become even more the case in retirement. When involvement with career ceases, when physical activities diminish with age, and when many other activities and busy trappings of life fade, relationships can take on an even more central role in our happiness.

Retirement is a major transition that has the capacity to threaten and challenge our relationships. Many people, in thinking of their retirement, fail to factor in what their retirement will do to their relationships. The message here is that in considering retirement, we should be sure to put enough emphasis on planning for the health and continuity of the primary relationships in our lives.

Indeed, an ideal retirement might be one that allows the primary relationships in one's life to develop even beyond their existing state. Some authors believe later life is an ideal time for us to develop in ways that are difficult to achieve in youth. Retirement may be the time to nurture and support the development of important relationships. It can be a time when people, no longer consumed by career concerns, can learn to "put the relationship first," and a time when they can learn to foster intimacy. Retirement can be a time when relationships can achieve both new depths of intimacy and new heights of joy.

Guiding Values and Life-Organizing Principles

One of the things that makes for a successful retirement is a sensible set of values. The Delany sisters are a powerful example of people who formulated an early set of values and principles that enabled them to succeed in life and work and also served them well into being centenarians. Their books stand as evidence of two people who led thoughtful lives adhering to principles formulated early in their lives, largely directed by their parents, that enabled them to succeed and be happy.

The Book of Everyday Wisdom is solid evidence that the Delany sisters had well thought out and time-tested values. Forged in hard times in the south, and expanded and revised as they went along life's trail, the sisters consistently followed a principled path. Sadie put it this way:

> So you want to live to be 100. Well, start with this: No smoking, no drinking, no chewing. And always clean your plate. . . .

40

Well, you can drink a little bit, but not too much. . . .

We get up with the sun, and the first thing we do is exercise.
God gave you only one body, so you better be nice to it. Exercise,
because if you don't, by the time you're our age, you'll be pushing
up daisies.[34]

In ways practical, intellectual, and spiritual, the sisters were
determined to lead a principled life—and they did. Several
of their life principles were relevant to successful retirement:
leading a frugal and non materialistic lifestyle, helping and
caring for others, lifelong habits of good diet and health, and a
strong sense of religion and spirituality.

Thriftiness and a Non-Materialistic Lifestyle

From their earliest years the sisters were encouraged by
their parents to value self-reliance. Their ethic also included
working hard, finding a respectable way to make a living,
prizing education, helping those less fortunate, and living a
frugal non-material life style. The sisters valued things other
than wealth and worldly possessions. They both worked
hard all their lives and yet never made extensive amounts
of money nor tried to. Ironically when they died they left
more than one million dollars to the St. Augustine's School,
largely the proceeds from their books. They both died in their
modest house in Mount Vernon New York, a house in which
they lived simply for almost 40 years. They made their own
soap, furnished the house with used furnishings, eschewed
modern conveniences, like the telephone, and cooked their
own meals. While they seemed interested in bettering the
quality and experience of their lives, they seemed uninterested
in technology and modern appliances. They were committed

to living frugally as a principle and did so even when they had money. They shared what they had with others less fortunate, and valued people over material possessions.

A large amount of research shows the Delany sisters had it right. Money by itself will not guarantee happiness. Research has shown that in comparing different cultures, societies, and individuals, there is little relationship between the money people have and their happiness.[35] We acknowledge that there is a certain level of income that is necessary to meet basic needs, but beyond that level the Delany sisters understood that little real happiness comes from simply accumulating more material goods. In fact, one of the Delany sister's words of advice quoted in their *Book of Everyday Wisdom* was this: "cut back on your possessions. The more you own the more time you waste taking care of things."[36] Modern society beams the message at all of us that the more we own the happier we will be. There is ample research to indicate this is not the case. It is hard to stand up to the constant barrage of messages telling us we need one more thing to be happy. The Delany sisters' strong family values helped them see beyond these specious claims. They seemed to always understand that the greatest joys could come from the simplest things:

> I found joy in so many different things. My friends and neighbors. My church. And I dearly loved my flowers and vegetables. . . . I love my garden so much that I would stay out there all day long if Sadie let me. That's what I mean by creating joy in your life. We all have to do it for ourselves.[37]

The message to all of us is to think about what will bring satisfaction in our later years. Money may not be as important to us as we think it is.

Helping and Caring for Others

A central guiding value for the Delany sisters was helping and caring for others. Even though they both achieved some level of material success, they never used that success only for themselves, but also to help others. From Bessie's early days as a dentist helping to care for the poor, to Sadie's weekly visits to the hospital to visit someone with no family, they continually made choices that would help others, even at some financial cost to themselves. It is an illustration of their values that, in reviewing her life, Sadie said the thing she was most proud of was using her educational talent to save the life of her ailing niece who was dying of pellagra.

Even their decision that Bessie should retire was based on a desire to care for their mother. This decision led to less money in retirement, but the Delany sisters never questioned that it needed to be done, and never regretted doing it. The sisters adopted their father's values of caring and community, and found that through giving to others, they achieved a life deeply satisfying to themselves. As we will discuss later, many people experience a shift from success to significance in their later years. For the Delany sisters no shift was necessary; they understood throughout their lives that the value of good relationships and close family ties and helping others were more important than accumulating wealth and material possessions.

Health Matters — Take Care of Yourself

Studies of retirement show that one significant factor related to happiness in later life is a person's health. The Delany sisters were fortunate to enjoy excellent health throughout their lives. Their long lives with good health illustrate a change that is occurring broadly throughout our society. As described in the introduction to this chapter, people today are not only living much longer, but are living many more years in good health.

The Delany sisters did not take their health for granted. They paid attention to it and worked on it. Perhaps because Sadie taught nutrition, they were always very conscious of what they ate. They were proud of never having smoked and found it hard to understand those who did. They carefully planned their diet to include many fruits and vegetables, and they exercised daily. In short, they followed a few simple precepts that most of us know, but that few of us have the discipline to maintain.

The message for successful retirement here is simple: Continued attention to good health habits will pay off. Even though many of us find it hard to eat well and exercise daily, developing good habits in this regard is even more important than ever before because of our increased chances of living to a very old age.

Religion and Spirituality

As daughters of an Episcopalian minister, and growing up at a religious school, religion played a guiding role in the Delany sisters' lives. Both sisters were spiritual and spoke often of what was the right thing to do from their religious perspective, sometimes joking about what would get them into heaven. Throughout their books there is little discussion of the formal trappings of religion, but a great deal of attention is paid to the central concepts of caring for others, treating others well, forgiveness, and respect for both others and one's self, and these core concepts played a guiding role in everything they did. They took these ideas to heart in a deep and enduring way.

There is much research to suggest that those with a deep set of spiritual values live a more satisfying retirement and perhaps even a longer life. For example, one study found that those who described themselves as "very" religious reported they were happier than those who described themselves as only "somewhat" or "not at all" religious.[38] Another study found that individuals who were more religious actually lived longer than those who were less religious.[39] It is not completely clear what causes this effect. For example, religious individuals as compared to less religious individuals are less likely to smoke and less likely to drink, and both of these factors may extend lifespan. They also may have more of a social support system, and someone to look in on them or call them if they are sick, to encourage them to get medical care, or even help them get to a doctor or hospital. Any or all of these factors may be involved in the greater longevity found among those who report themselves to be more religious. Whatever the cause, it does seem to be the case that some sense of spirituality and religiosity may be associated with a longer and more satisfying life.[40] The Delany sisters' lives are an illustration of this concept.

Personal Characteristics

Perhaps one of the most critical factors determining happiness in retirement is a person's attitudes and personal characteristics. The Delany sisters are a wonderful model in this regard. They seemed to have a positive attitude about everything, even when faced with obstacles and adversity. Their energy, enthusiasm, and optimism helped them through situations that would have led many people to give up or to become permanently resentful. Perhaps the most difficult and enduring challenge they faced was racism and prejudice. As they describe the many situations they confronted, their ability to remain positive is truly impressive. They may have gotten angry but they never became bitter. As Sadie put it, they believed that "bitterness won't change a thing. It will ruin [your life]. If we'd been bitter and full of hate we'd never have lived the pleasant life we've lived. Sometimes we get mad, but there is big difference between anger and bitterness."[41]

In addition to their positive outlook, another personal characteristic that served them well was their personal discipline. They established and maintained regular positive habits throughout their lives. Their regular diet, yoga and daily exercise, daily letter writing, and even watching the news, were signs of discipline and order. All of their major decisions seemed to have been made carefully and thoughtfully. When they chose to enter their careers, they needed advanced education, and they knew this would require getting a job and saving money. Each of them carried out a plan to thoughtfully achieve the goals they had established. Their subsequent decisions to move to different homes, Bessie's retirement to take care of their mother, and Sadie's retirement, were all made with the same thoughtfulness.

In our review and analysis of the factors leading to happiness, we have found that one guideline for enduring personal satisfaction is to establish high but achievable goals and then work hard to meet those goals. The Delany sisters did this throughout their lives. They followed their father's advice that the way to make a better world was to work hard and do your best at everything you did. Both sisters set high goals for their education and their careers, as well as for the way they conducted themselves every day, and then worked hard to achieve those goals. Whenever things were difficult they stuck to the family values of working harder and doing your best. The Delany sisters had a positive and optimistic outlook on life right up until the very end. Even after the age of 100 they stayed enthusiastic and interested in all that life had to offer.

> Most folks think getting older means giving up, not trying anything new. Well, we don't agree with that. As long as you can see each day as a chance for something new to happen, something you never expected before, you will stay young. Why, we don't feel that we're 105 and 103 — we feel half that old! Even after a century of living, we haven't tried everything. We've only just started.[42]

The Delanys' lives illustrate that a set of positive values and core personal attributes can lead to successful lives that carry over into happy and successful retirement years. If the personal characteristics described here are inborn personality characteristics, then some fortunate people would have these characteristics, and be likely to have successful and positive retirements, while others who were not born so lucky would be doomed to a far lower likelihood of success. But the good news is that these characteristics are not inborn and inevitable; they can be learned. In his book *Learned Optimism*, Martin Seligman makes the point that a pattern of positive outlook can be learned by early experience, and is something an individual can strive to achieve.[43] Timothy Miller makes the same point in his book, *How to Want What You Have*.[44] Many other authors of advice and self-help books have made the same argument. Optimism and a positive attitude can be learned.

A great deal has been written about how to form good habits. With motivation and effort, all of us can establish good habits that will serve us well and enhance our late life satisfaction, such as habits of eating well and exercising. And if we realize the importance of doing so, we can develop a pattern of setting ourselves achievable goals and then working toward them. In short, we can develop some of the attitudes and characteristics that led the Delany sisters to such long and positive lives in their many years of retirement.

3

Lee Iacocca:
Money Isn't Enough

Planning for Retirement: The Focus on Finances

Many people who are approaching retirement have not done much planning for it. If they have done any planning, chances are that what they've thought about are mostly the financial aspects of retirement. We've interviewed many people about retirement, and this is the kind of thing we hear people say:

> We didn't really think about what life would be like after Joe retired. He was approaching the standard retirement age, and getting more and more fed up with his job. He had a new boss that he really didn't like. We started thinking maybe it was time for him to retire. We spent quite a bit of time figuring

out whether we could handle it financially. We looked at our savings, calculated what his retirement income would be, and even made out what we thought was a realistic budget. What we didn't think about at all was what it would take for us to be really happy in retirement. Sure, we had a vague image of what life would be like. But mostly we thought "we won't have to do THAT any more." We didn't really think through what we DID want to do.

This statement reflects what often happens in American society when people begin to think about retirement. They spend some time doing financial planning—maybe even a lot of time. But they don't spend much time thinking about the non-financial aspects of retirement. Financial planning for retirement is certainly important, but it's not enough. Research has shown that other aspects of retirement—what we call the "personal side of retirement"—is equally important. And those non-financial considerations are all too often ignored.

This excessive focus on financial preparation for retirement is apparent everywhere. A review of newspaper, television and magazine advertisements about retirement shows that the overwhelming majority of them are about retirement funds. It's even true on the Internet. Recently we conducted an informal analysis of Internet sites by searching for sites on the topic of retirement. About 90 percent of the sites we found had to do with mutual funds, equity funds, and financial planning. And almost all of the remaining sites seemed to be about buying land in Florida! Only a tiny percentage of sites addressed the non-financial aspects of retirement.

But when we look at what actually makes people satisfied with their retirement, we find that finances have remarkably little to do with satisfaction. Beyond a certain minimum financial need, more money doesn't seem to lead to more happiness.[1]

A striking example of this is Lee Iacocca, the former President of Ford Motor Company and later Chairman of Chrysler Corporation. When he retired in 1992 at age 68, Iacocca should have been poised for a wonderful retirement. He had reached the pinnacle of success. He had turned Chrysler around from a company in debt to a thriving company, with his introduction of the enormously successful mini-van concept. He had been earning a million dollars a year, and owned a multi-million dollar house in California and a villa in Europe. He had written two best-selling books, and was in demand on the lecture circuit to the tune of $60,000 per lecture. Describing himself as a member of the "working rich," Lee Iacocca certainly had no financial problems.

Despite all his wealth, two years after he retired, Iacocca was describing his retirement as a failure. What happened? How could someone with so much money, prestige, and power, be so miserable in retirement? If money is a good predictor of happiness in retirement, what went wrong? There is much we can learn from the Lee Iacocca story.

Life After Work

The Backstory

If there was anyone who should have been positioned for an enjoyable retirement after a highly successful career, it should have been Lee Iacocca. He was born Lido Anthony Iacocca on October 15, 1924, in Allentown, Pennsylvania, just a few years before the Great Depression. The son of Italian immigrants, he grew up in an area that was mostly Dutch, and he was often picked on for being different. Even as a youth, Iacocca had enormous drive and energy. As a teenager, he worked 16-hour days on the weekends at a fruit market, earning two dollars a day, plus all the fruit he could eat. Later, he became friendly with a man who owned a car dealership. By the time he was 15, he had decided to go into the automobile business, and from that time forward "all my energies were directed to doing just that."[2] During the Depression, the Iacocca family's hard-won financial stability eroded. "The Depression turned me into a materialist," he recounts in his autobiography, and describes his attitude as a college student: "I wasn't interested in a snob degree; I was after the bucks."[3]

In 1939, he had rheumatic fever, which later prevented him from serving in the Army. He went to Lehigh University in Bethlehem, Pennsylvania, where he completed college in eight straight semesters. He graduated in 1945, and got a fellowship to attend Princeton, where he earned a master's degree in engineering in 1946.

The Ford Years

After graduating from Princeton, Iacocca got a job at Ford Motor Company, beginning as a student engineer.

However, after nine months in a training program, he found that engineering no longer interested him. He liked working with people more than machines, and decided that sales or marketing was where the action was. He got an entry-level job selling Fords at an office in Chester Pennsylvania. Although he later admitted having had no natural talent as a salesperson, Iacocca dedicated himself to mastering the art of selling. His talent was recognized and he became a zone manager and fleet representative, spending lots of time in the field working with dealers.

While working at the Ford sales office in Pennsylvania, he met his first wife, Mary McClearly, who was a receptionist in the nearby Ford assembly plant. They married on September 29, 1956, and stayed together for 27 years until Mary died of complications from diabetes in 1983. Iacocca and Mary had two daughters, Kathryn and Lia.

From the beginning, making money was a primary motivation for Iacocca. Charlie Beacham, a regional manager who was like a mentor to Iacocca during his early years in sales, used to say "Make money. Screw everything else. This is a profit-making system, boy. The rest is frills."[4] Recalling an early promotion, Iacocca said, "It wasn't prestige or power I wanted. It was money."[5]

Later on, however, when he had plenty of money, it seemed that power and prestige did become a driving force for him. Describing how he felt when he became president of Ford, he spoke of how he "certainly enjoyed the prestige and the power of my position."[6]

By 1960 he had become general manager of the Ford division and vice-president of the company. Iacocca's increasing power within the company was hastened by his introduction of the dramatically successful Ford Mustang. He quickly rose through the ranks, and was named president of Ford on December 10, 1970.[7]

It is difficult to imagine the scale on which Iacocca operated. The company he worked for was huge. In 1970, when he became President of Ford, it was the second largest company in the world, with over 432,000 employees and a total payroll of more than $3.5 billion. Total sales for 1970 were $14.9 billion. One example illustrates the scale at which they operated. In a cost cutting effort, redesigning a fender to make each car two inches shorter allowed more cars to fit into each freight train and saved the company 2.5 million dollars in freight costs.[8]

Looking back on his years as general manager of the Ford Division, Iacocca described it as "fire in the belly time," with a combination of hard work and big dreams, and the happiest period of his life. In 1968, at age 44, he was a vice-president at Ford and driving toward becoming its next president. "In those days," he says, "I was in a mad rush to the top."[9] Reflecting on why anyone would want to be president and want to work so hard, he said "So he can say 'Hey, I made it to the top. I accomplished something.' "[10]

Indeed, Iacocca had enormous energy. As president of Ford, he continued to put in huge numbers of hours at work, and he said "I loved my job, even though many people viewed it as the kind of position that grinds you up and kills you off. But I never saw it that way. To me, it was sheer excitement."[11] But he did slow down a bit as he grew older. By the time he got to be president of Ford, he "had to learn a different style of operating" because he "no longer had the stamina of the Mustang years, when I thought nothing of grabbing a hamburger for dinner and staying at the office until midnight."[12] He was also a man with enormous self-confidence, who characterized himself as impatient and outspoken, and who was described in a June 1982 front page story in The Wall Street Journal as "a man with an ego as big as all outdoors."[13]

In 1978, eight years after becoming president of Ford Motor Company, Lee Iacocca was fired. He had worked his way up from humble beginnings to running one of the largest corporations in the world. After being fired, he metaphorically likened this experience to reaching the top of Mt. Everest, and then being kicked off the mountain.

Iacocca had worked for Ford his entire life. He was totally dedicated to the company. The fall from grace was sudden and devastating. He wasn't really prepared for the firing, and hadn't told his family that it was likely to happen.

But there had been plenty of warnings that he chose to ignore. More than two years earlier, Henry Ford had launched a long investigation of Iacocca that one friend described as a "witch-hunt," trying to uncover anything in either his private or professional life that could be used against him.[14] His friends and colleagues were cross-examined for any hints of problems, he found his phone calls being monitored, and he and suspected his desk was being searched. Iacocca described Henry Ford as engaged in a "month-by-month premeditated plan to destroy me."[15] Closer to the time he was finally fired, Henry Ford began doing things behind Iacocca's back and making decisions that undercut him. And in the months leading up to the firing, Henry Ford had restructured senior management by creating new positions that effectively demoted Iacocca from second in command to third, and then to fourth.

All of this was having an emotional impact, not only on Iacocca, but also on his beloved wife Mary. As a diabetic, stress was very bad for her. In fact, Iacocca says that stress was involved with all the bad things that happened to Mary regarding her health. Mary had her first heart attack less than three months after he was fired from Ford. In the late 1970s and early 1980s, Mary had two heart attacks and a stroke, each event following a period of great stress in her husband's career.[16]

With all these hints that he might be let go, and with the negative impact it was having on his family, why didn't Iacocca quit or look for another job? In part, it was the natural human tendency to avoid and deny problems, to just keep hoping they will go away and things will get better. In part it was pride. "It might have been pride, it might have been stupidity, but I was not going to crawl out of there with my tail between my legs."[17] In part, he just couldn't imagine working anywhere else. And in part, he admits, he was greedy. He liked the perks and the status, and he found it "almost impossible to walk away from an annual income of $970,000."[18] Since his youth, money had always been important to Iacocca. After college he set himself a goal of becoming a millionaire. From his early years at Ford, he was envious of people who earned more than he did, and throughout his career the driving force for him was money. The money was also important to him for the status it implied. For a couple of years in the 1970s, he and Henry Ford were listed as the two highest paid businessmen in America, and "my mother and father thought that was terrific, a real badge of honor."[19]

What upset him most about being fired was the public humiliation and the suffering it caused his family. He was angry with Henry Ford, who had stripped him of his leadership role in spite of his exemplary performance, and had fired him publicly before he had the opportunity to share the bad news with his family in private. "Even today, their pain is what stays with me," he recounts in the prologue to his autobiography.[20] Years later his most powerful memory of the experience was of his daughter Lia crying to him on the phone when she heard the news.

It was unclear exactly why he was fired. In one view, his brash, unorthodox manner led to his downfall. Others believed he was fired because he had done such a extraordinary job that Henry Ford started to fear Iacocca was trying to take over the company. Perhaps both views were correct. Either way, Henry Ford fired Lee Iacocca on October 15, 1978. Not surprisingly, Iacocca expressed no love for Henry Ford. In his 1984 autobiography, Iacocca painted a picture of Ford as a vengeful, unpredictable, autocratic, dictatorial, petty person who was paranoid about any potential threats to his power. He described the grandson of the company's founder as an "insecure spoiled brat."[21] He also accuses Ford of being a woman-hating chauvinist and playboy who never worked hard but only played hard.[22] He even went so far as to describe Ford as an "evil man."[23]

After his firing, one incident had an especially powerful impact on Iacocca. He was moving into an outlying office that had been provided for him until he found another job. His old office as President had been extraordinarily luxurious. It was the size of a grand hotel suite, with a private bathroom and living quarters. White coated executives were always on call to serve the Ford food that was flown in daily from all around the world.

His new office was strikingly different. It was located in a drab warehouse several miles from the executive headquarters. When he arrived, Iacocca found cracked linoleum on the floor, plastic coffee cups on the desk, and a coffee machine in the hall. His new office was little more than a cubicle with a small desk and a telephone. He said he felt like he was being exiled to Siberia. It made him "feel like shit."[24] He was filled with anger. He wrote that this final humiliation was much worse than being fired. When he left that makeshift office at the end of that first day, he never came back.

His arrival at the shabby warehouse office was a turning point for Iacocca. He briefly considered retirement, but he wasn't ready to "pack it all in" and "play golf for the rest of my life."[25] He decided to use the energy from his anger to do something productive. Chrysler Corporation was on the ropes and was looking for new leadership to turn the company around. They began to pursue Iacocca, whose reputation outside of Ford was still that of a powerful leader and strong innovator. Within a few months, he was hired as chairman of Chrysler Corporation and faced an enormous new set of responsibilities and challenges.

The Chrysler Years

Iacocca became CEO of Chrysler in September 1979. The Company's mounting problems threatened bankruptcy, and Iacocca needed to act fast. Iacocca mounted a brilliantly organized and successful campaign that culminated in securing a large government bail-out loan, totally reorganizing Chrysler, and initiating the development of innovative new products.

As president and chairman of the board of the floundering Chrysler Corporation, he secured the largest amount of federal financial assistance ever given to a private corporation at that time—a loan of 1.5 billion dollars.[26] There was great controversy about whether Congress should back such a loan to private industry, but finally, Congress approved the loan in 1980. Under Iacocca's leadership, Chrysler paid back the loan in 1983, seven years before it was due.[27] His dynamic leadership in the successful struggle to save the company, and thus the jobs of thousands of American autoworkers, made Iacocca a hero to many.

Iacocca hadn't known how deep Chrysler's financial difficulties were at the time he took the job, and if he did, he was to say later, he might never have taken it. Indeed, one of the difficult things for him, as he called old friends to ask them to join his team, was lying to himself about how bad the situation really was.

Much of his effort at Chrysler was salesmanship, though now at a higher level than ever before. First he had to sell Congress on the loan, and then he had to sell all the constituents on taking the cuts and losses they had to accept for the loan guarantees to take effect. The unions had to take pay cuts, suppliers had to cut costs and take partial payments, and the bankers had to extend payments, renegotiate loans, and take some losses. But Iacocca was a terrific salesman, and a seasoned combatant, battle-tested in adversity. In the end he pulled off the largest congressionally backed guaranteed loan in U.S. history. Testifying before Congress was a huge challenge. He was referred to as a witness, but was treated as a defendant. Hour after hour he sat in a box, television lights in his eyes, looking at committee members seated at a semicircular table a level above him. He had to respond to everything on the spot, while the senators and congressmen who were questioning him had staffers to check their facts and keep the flow of pointed questions coming. Many of the questions were hostile; some were more like speeches than questions. He said "it was murder." There were cartoons in the papers, editorials, and jokes on TV. He felt punished and humiliated: ". . . it was personal. It was pointed. And it was painful."[28] But in the end Congress approved the loan.

Then came the challenge of getting the unions, the banks, the suppliers, and a host of other constituents to agree to the required concessions. One story captures the size of this effort. As a condition of the loan, Iacocca had to get $655 million in concessions from 400 leading banks, and every single bank had to sign on to the deal or the whole thing would crumble. It took 22 task forces and months of arm-twisting and negotiating, but finally a deal was agreed to. The final closing took place at a single huge meeting that involved large groups of lawyers and over 10,000 individual documents. Stacked in a pile, they would have reached as high as a seven-story building, and the printing bill for the documents alone was almost two million dollars.[29]

Iacocca certainly was a master planner when it came to business. When he went to Chrysler, the first thing he found was that they needed better planning. People at Chrysler weren't even talking to each other, but were running separate fiefdoms. "People in engineering and manufacturing almost have to be sleeping together. These guys weren't even flirting!"[30] The corporate culture would need to change, if it was to survive. As CEO, Iacocca would have to craft a team from the disjointed roster he'd inherited.

As one example, when Iacocca arrived at Chrysler the company was producing excess cars kept in huge lots known as the "sales bank." Instead of building cars based on dealer orders, Chrysler built cars based on guesses and then tried to convince the dealers to buy them. This led to monthly sales to dealers in order to clear out the lots, and dealers began to wait for the sales, producing a giant guessing game that backed up the system even further. At one point the inventory reached 100,000 cars—which meant that over six hundred million dollars was just sitting in lots. Iacocca totally eliminated the system and instituted a procedure of planned production based on firm dealer commitments and careful analysis of future needs.

With cost cutting measures and new products, Iacocca led a turnaround at Chrysler. He found new sources of credit, trimmed operations, closed plants, and persuaded labor unions to accept layoffs and wage cuts. He then shifted the company's emphasis to fuel-efficient models and undertook an aggressive advertising campaign that included personal appearances on television commercials. By 1981 Chrysler showed a small profit, and three years later it announced record profits of more than $2.4 billion.[31] As profits mounted, he diversified into new areas. Chrysler bought the Gulfstream Aerospace Corp., which was later sold. In 1984, he launched the enormously popular minivan, leading the way in a new concept that soon would be copied everywhere in the American automobile industry. In 1987, Chrysler bought the struggling American Motors Corporation and its Jeep line of four wheel drive vehicles, which became highly profitable for Chrysler.[32]

Iacocca's public exposure while securing the Chrysler loan gave him a public persona uncharacteristic of the head of a large car company. He became a national figure. His willingness to be involved in the ad campaigns for cars like the mini-van was unusual. He appeared widely on TV advertisements for Chrysler with his well-known slogan: "If you can find a better car, buy it!"

He became so popular that he flirted with the Democratic Party presidential nomination in 1984 and again in 1988, and large sums of money were raised on his behalf. His autobiography, *Iacocca* (1984), and a second book, *Talking Straight,* (1988), were best sellers.[33]

In the late 1980s, Chrysler once again ran into financial difficulties. Iacocca launched a major cost cutting campaign in 1989, lopping off 11,000 salaried workers, and generating savings of $4 billion. He started a giant new vehicle program costing $46.5 billion annually over five years. These moves paid off, as Chrysler returned to profitability in 1992, when nine-month earnings hit a surprising $312 million.

As Iacocca was approaching retirement at Chrysler, he had many other opportunities that he chose not to pursue. In fact, the opportunities that were presented to Iacocca would read like a list of dream jobs, with the highest prestige one could imagine. Tex Colbert, the former chairman of Chrysler, approached him to be president of Harvard. Then when Senator John Heinz was killed in an airplane crash in 1991, Robert Casey, the Governor of Pennsylvania, wanted to appoint him to Heinz's vacant senate seat. Congressman John Murtha said he would get Iacocca two committee memberships so he would have some clout.

The only problem was that I would have to run for reelection six months after I was appointed. Then I got a call from the "ragin' Cajun," James Carville, who said the Democrats wouldn't support me when I ran in the fall unless I did certain things. He told me what I had to think and do because of the polls. I said, The hell with you guys. So I turned the Governor down.[34]

Iacocca was even approached about being baseball commissioner. George Steinbrenner, owner of the Yankees and an old friend, and Bill Bartholomay of the Atlanta Braves, head of the commissioner selection process, came to talk to him about it. But once again he decided that he wanted to stay at Chrysler.

During his time at Chrysler, Iacocca experienced difficulties and trauma in his personal life. In 1983 Iacocca's wife of 27 years, Mary McClearly, died of complications from diabetes, after many years of struggling with the disease. He soon remarried, but that marriage, which he termed a "rebound marriage" failed in 1987.[35] In 1991, the year before he retired from Chrysler, he married his third wife, Darrien Earle.

Iacocca's Early Views on Retirement

It seems that Iacocca did not think very deeply about retirement before he himself retired. In the autobiography he wrote eight years before he retired, he hardly mentions retirement, but what he does say is quite revealing. When describing his reaction after he was fired from Ford, he says he wondered if he should "pack it all in and retire….I was fifty-four years old. I had already accomplished a great deal. I was financially secure. I could afford to play golf for the rest of my life."[36] Retirement, to Iacocca, seemed synonymous with not doing anything productive.

He also disliked mandatory retirement and thought it was a terrible idea. "I've always felt it was ridiculous that when a guy reaches sixty-five, no matter what shape he's in, we retire him instantly."[37] He thought that older executives had learned a lot over the years and it was foolish to waste their wisdom and experience. "If you can still come to work at age sixty-five and do a good job, why should you have to leave?"[38]

If Iacocca thought that mandatory retirement was a bad idea, he thought that early retirement was even worse:

> I've seen too many executives announce that they will retire at fifty-five. Then when they turn fifty-five they feel compelled to carry it through. . . . Many of these guys fall apart when they retire. They have become used to the tough grind, with lots of excitement and high risks — big successes and big failures. Then they suddenly find themselves playing golf and going home for lunch. I've seen a lot of men die only a few months after they retire. Sure, working can kill you. But so can not working."[39]

It is interesting how much Iacocca's comments forecast his own retirement experience. In his second book, written four years later, he did make a few brief references to his own anticipated retirement, but they were very negative. "Once I finish up at Chrysler, I suppose I could load up the car and head for Florida, where I could sit by the pool and play golf every day. But I'm not built that way. I have to work. What are you going to do with your life if you don't work?"[40]

Later he was asked about his impending retirement in an interview for *Fortune* magazine in September 1992. Iacocca said: "it's a good time to be retiring because everything I wanted to do is finished."[41] But when asked how he felt about his successes at Ford and Chrysler, he said "I feel tired."[42] And when he was asked the question, "What's retirement going to be like for you?" He replied: "After 46 years in the mines? It's going to be traumatic. I'll probably wake up the first morning … and wonder what to do with myself."[43] Later, he did describe some of the things he wanted to do, but these never seemed very specific.

> "I have a lot of things that I haven't had a chance to do in education, maybe even health care. To see kids not even getting a good grade school education is a tragedy. I think we all have to do something. I'm national head of the PTA this year (1992), trying to get parents involved."[44]

Iacocca said there were certainly some things he was not going to miss when he retired. He talked about the loss of privacy he faced after doing TV ads and writing two books. He described "people coming up to you and wanting to talk and wanting autographs," and said "I will not miss any of that. Believe me, that is a difficult thing to cope with."[45]

He also said that he didn't care how the public remembers him. He was concerned only about how his kids and family and friends remember him. "The public at large—I have no particular legacy that I want to be remembered by. I enjoyed life. I did what I wanted to do. I'm done earning. I'm at the point in life where I've got to figure out how to give the money away rather than how to earn it."[46]

Iacocca's Retirement

Iacocca retired as CEO of Chrysler Corporation on December 31, 1992 at age 68. It was the peak of Chrysler's recovery. There were some rumors that he may have been forced out, but he denied that. He said his stepping down as CEO was based on an agreement he made with Chrysler's board several years earlier.

He states emphatically that he was not forced out at Chrysler, but chose to retire voluntarily. "This story that I went out of Chrysler kicking and screaming, that's pure myth. That's absolutely wrong."[47] Given the candor with which he described his life, including his firing from Ford, it is reasonable to believe him when he says that his retirement from Chrysler was voluntary. Assuming his retirement was voluntary, what were the reasons he gave for retiring?

By 1992, he had said to himself, "Gee everything is in place. . . . I had gone through the pain of integrating American Motors. Minivans were hot . . . the Chrysler Technology Center was done . . . I had cut four billion dollars out of our operating costs."[48] Iacocca's attitude toward retirement was changing. He was ready to accept it now. "I really wanted to retire. I had turned 68, and I was getting tired. I'd done everything."[49]

His third wife had moved to California and he began to make plans to join her there. He also said he wanted to be free of having every hour of his life scheduled: "That's the reason I got out of Chrysler. I was in good health, I could have stayed a long time. It wasn't so much the worldwide travel, it was carrying a card in my pocket that had every hour of my life scheduled."[50]

Careful planning for retirement involves several things. One is having a good understanding of the reasons you want to retire. Another is having carefully thought about the things you want to do in retirement. Iacocca was vague in both areas. Looking back later, he seemed to realize that he had not planned well for his own retirement. In a 1996 interview, he said this on the subject: "I wasn't ready for it. Most people aren't, especially CEOs."[51] During the interview, he did not describe things he had planned to do in retirement or looked forward to doing. Instead, he said, "I had to find something to do with my life."

Post Retirement Years

Iacocca's retirement did not turn out well. In a 1996 *Fortune* magazine article he admitted, "I flunked retirement." The article headline put it this way: "Lee Iacocca says his three years of retirement have been more stressful than his 47 years in the auto business."[52] After retiring, Iacocca moved to California to be with his wife. What he didn't know was that she was about to divorce him. Iacocca was unaware that his marriage was falling apart, and did not seem to have a real understanding of what happened in the deterioration of their relationship. He and his wife seemed to want different things from life. She wanted to live in California, but his consulting work kept him in Detroit even after his "retirement." The marriage lasted only three and a half years. Even though he bought a beautiful home in California with the intention of moving there to be with her—it was already too late. All he could say was, "I wish I knew what went wrong."[53]

Retiring from his lifelong career, moving to a new state, losing his support relationships, and trying to figure out what to do next with his life was just too much all at once. He said "if I had to give somebody advice, it would be to hang on to something familiar: at least your house and your wife."[54] Iacocca lost both.

Referring later to living in California without his third wife, he said "I'm here by myself now, but still optimistic. People ask me why I'm still working so hard. I tell them that without that, and without my kids and grandkids, I'd lose it — I'd have nothing." He was alone and did not like being alone. Iacocca said, "I don't want to eat by myself, sleep by myself. It's OK to have some private moments, but if you're alone [your] whole life is a private moment. You'd better go see somebody because you'll go crazy. When you're alone you're alone. Period."[55] Despite how social and gregarious Iacocca's professional life was, he found it hard to make new friends and develop new intimate relationships.

Iacocca also said he had not been successful in trying slow down and smell the roses. "I have too much going on. I am bogged down in paper. . . . It has got to stop. . . . I want to simplify my life. That's almost a full-time job."[56] And when asked how he spent his time in retirement, Iacocca said: "I exercise about an hour every morning. Then I read the *New York Times* from cover to cover. I do the crossword puzzle every day . . . I play a little tennis"[57]

Later Activities After His Retirement

Lee Iacocca did keep busy after his retirement. He remained involved in a number of business activities, but these activities seem, for the most part, unrewarding and unfulfilling. They seem a pale image of the excitement during his pre-retirement years. After retiring as CEO he continued to serve on Chrysler's board and was chairman of the board's executive committee. In 1995, shortly after his retirement from Chrysler, he became involved in a failed takeover bid for the company. He says he played a minor role in that, and let someone use his name without paying enough attention to what was happening. But it was an unpleasant experience. *Time* magazine described it as an abortive bid to take over Chrysler that "ended in a fiasco of lawsuits, not to mention accusations of treachery and avarice by his former colleagues."[58]

Ronald Perelman, whose New World Communications board he served on, built him a plush office. He invested in a couple of businesses. One, started by a next door neighbor, was a chain of fast food restaurants called Koo Koo Roo that served healthy foods such as skinless chicken, salads and steamed vegetables. Iacocca was very enthusiastic about it and thought it would become a national chain. It turned out he was overly optimistic.

Iacocca also continued his involvement with the Iacocca Institute, which had been founded in 1988 at his alma mater Lehigh University. The institute was dedicated to increasing the global competitiveness of American business. Over the years Iacocca helped raise a lot of money for this venture. But given his many connections, this may not have required a great deal of time or energy or on his part.

Iacocca also remained in demand as a public speaker. He was getting 60,000 dollars for speaking 30 minutes. His books and syndicated column together generated 15 million dollars. He put that with another 15 million dollars of his own, and dedicated it all to diabetic research through a foundation he had founded in memory of his wife Mary, who had died of diabetes in 1983.

Even though he had written two very successful books, Iacocca did not want to write another one. Publishers wanted to give him over a million dollars to write a book but he said he wasn't interested. It isn't clear why he felt that way. With the extensive resources at his command it would have been relatively easy to continue his writing career. This was an opportunity for continued productivity that Iacocca chose not to pursue.

In 1996, he started EV Global Motors, a company to market electric bicycles made in Taiwan. A February 1999 *Time* magazine article claimed that "Iacocca is alive and well at 73." It quoted Iacocca as saying "I think I have one vision left in me before I die, and it's electric."[59] According to the article, friends said his involvement in this project "has rejuvenated a man who told *Fortune* magazine he had flunked retirement." He has since become heavily involved in the green car movement and has started a company called Lido Motors to develop small electric vehicles. To date, these projects have not provided Iacocca or his investors with much in the way of recognition or financial gain.

More successful has been Iacocca's connection with Olivio Premium Products. Founded in 1993 and run by his son-in-law, profits from the company's sales of olive oil based products benefit the Iacocca Foundation for diabetes research. While his name has been associated with many charitable causes over the years, the Iacocca Foundation remains consistently high profile. In 2004, when diabetes research in mice showed promise for success with humans, the Foundation launched the "Join Lee Now" initiative to raise another 11.5 million dollars to fund that work. Chrysler was drawn into the campaign, pledging one dollar for each car sold while Iacocca appeared in their new advertisements.

It is interesting and surprising that in 2005, at the age of 81, Iacocca once again reappeared in a series of television advertisements for Chrysler cars. These ads are very odd in that they draw upon images, slogans, and ideas from the Iacocca period and try to connect them to a younger generation. In one advertisement, the youthful rap artist SnoopDogg and an elderly Iacocca are playing golf, and the ad suggests that the two of them agree on very little, but they both agree on the power and superiority of Chrysler cars. In all of the ads Iacocca repeats the old slogan he made famous more than twenty years earlier: "If you can find a better car, buy it!" It is hard to believe that there is a large audience that would remember either Iacocca or the slogan.

No matter what one thinks of these ads and their effectiveness, they do imply that the essential Iacocca image is connected to what he did at, and for, Chrysler. All this supports the idea that the Chrysler period was the peak time for Iacocca—one that could not be matched by anything since.

What the Lee Iacocca Story Tells Us

Money by Itself Is Not Enough

Making money had always been a primary motivation for Iacocca, and he had plenty of money when he retired. But this did not lead to happiness for him in retirement. The message for the rest of us seems to be this: It is fine to plan for your finances in retirement, and indeed important to do so. But recognize that money by itself will not guarantee happiness in retirement. Other things—such as our relationships, and continued involvement in activities that are significant and meaningful to us—are important as well.

As we contemplate retirement, it is important to consider those aspects of what we call the "personal side of retirement." The simple fact is that finances do not relate closely to happiness. When we stop to think about it, most of us realize this is true. We probably know some people who don't seem to have much money but seem very happy, and others who have lots of money but don't seem very happy at all. If we reflect on our own lives, we may discover the same thing. For many of us, some of the happiest times of our lives came when we didn't have much money at all. And when we did get more money, or that raise we had been waiting for, or the bigger house we craved, it did not really increase our happiness as much as we thought it would. For most of us, an honest reflection suggests that our happiness may have depended on lots of things, but the relationship between our happiness and our financial situation was an indirect one, at best.

A substantial amount of research supports the conclusion that a person's financial situation has little relation to his or her overall level of happiness. David Myers is a social scientist who has carefully analyzed the research on happiness and life satisfaction that has been carried out over the past 50 years. In his book *The Pursuit of Happiness*[60] he states that wealth bears only a minimal relation to life satisfaction, and "once beyond poverty, further economic growth does not appreciably improve human morale."[61] Martin Seligman, a professor at the University of Pennsylvania, describes additional research that comes to the same conclusion in his book *Authentic Happiness*.[62]

Although these research findings relate to life satisfaction in general and not specifically in retirement, our work with people who have retired leads us to the same conclusion. We interviewed many individuals who had retired. Just as in the research described by Myers, we found that beyond a certain minimum level, the financial situation of retired individuals did not have much of a relationship to their happiness.

Iacocca's story illustrates these points. Money was always important to Iacocca. He said that even from early on he knew that he was "after the bucks." His early mentor had told him to make money and forget everything else, and he accepted that message without question. But money never seemed to make him happy. His happiest periods were when he was working on a worthy challenge. By his own admission he achieved his goal of personal wealth early in his career. The interesting point is that he didn't seem to understand that his relentless pursuit of money would not make him happy.

The most striking message from the Lee Iacocca story is that money is not enough to have a satisfying retirement. Finances are what people talk about most, worry about most, and plan about most when they consider retirement. However, financial security by itself is not enough, and indeed a person's financial situation in retirement may bear little relation to his or her happiness in retirement.

Language Matters

The Iacocca story also illustrates that the language we use to describe a thing is important. Language gives a significant shape to an idea. As we use certain language to describe something, our description comes back to us and adds to the shape of the idea itself. This is especially true of the concept of retirement. The word retirement implies stopping or ending something. It does not focus on what you will be doing—rather what you are going to stop doing. An example of a language change that produced a perception change was when our country changed the name of the "Department of War" to the "Department of Defense." This really gave the country a new way to think about the entire issue of national security. Some would argue that language is just "window dressing." We think it is far more important. It leads one to perceive a thing in a different light.

The idea that language gives shape to our perception applies to Iacocca and retirement. The language he used for retirement was drawn from a very old vocabulary. It was a language of "either/or"—either you are working or you are "done" and "finished" and the significant work of your life is "stopped." In the old industrial language of retirement, you worked until you were "worn out." There was no expectation, and thus no language, to describe another stage of exciting and productive life, different from your work years. Iacocca seems to have the old notion in his mind more strongly than any newer notion of a productive transition to new and exciting things. Whenever he talked about retirement he used images like playing golf every day, sitting by the pool, and packing up the car and heading for Florida. These were very negative images for him. He saw retirement as a transition into a kind of blank and empty space. Work was the thing, in his eyes, that gave meaning to life. He had a very limited conception of what "work" was. For him, work involved climbing the ladder of the corporate world. One gets the feeling that if he had a different way of talking and thinking about this, it might have redirected his energy along lines of a more positive transition.

Iacocca's language and conception for retirement was that of the industrial age. He lived in a macho, man's world (and language) of competition and drive, of takeovers and downsizing, of the players and the vanquished. You are either "in" or you are "out." It is not a language of, nor reality of, redefinition or transformation. He forecast it well when asked about retirement while he was at Chrysler: "After 46 years in the mines? It's going to be traumatic!"[63] And it was. We feel it is too bad that this creative and energetic person did not have a language that would have helped create and shape some of the exciting possibilities that were open to him. This stage of his life was not really about "quitting." It was about a major life transformation. But nothing in his language would tell you (or him) that.

To be fair, Iacocca did find some interesting things to do in retirement. But they seem to lack a unifying theme and a vision worthy of his intelligence and his creativity. In all the books and articles we read he seemed to have trouble articulating positive intentions for his life after retirement. He used very negative language to describe retirement—and it turned out to be a very negative experience for him.

What we can learn from this is that we need to start using different ways to talk about retirement that do not carry negative images of only termination and loss. Unfortunately the word "retirement" in our culture does carry with it the image of stopping everything productive and doing nothing meaningful with one's life. In thinking about our own retirement, and talking about it both to ourselves and to others, we should describe it as a constructive transition to a new stage of our lives, a stage that can be exciting, productive and fulfilling. We all make a choice by the words we use to describe something. It is our belief that better language has the potential to lead to a better conception of retirement itself.

Rethinking Our Goals

In Lee Iacocca's own words, his overarching goal in life was to make money. That is a common theme in the business world. While still in college, Iacocca had set himself a goal of becoming a millionaire. In Iacocca's case, his rise to the top was so fast that he had more money than he knew what to do with by the Ford years. His salary plus options at Ford had him earning almost a million dollars a year in the mid-1970s. Unless a person is exceedingly greedy (and we are not suggesting that Iacocca was), beyond a certain level making more money doesn't bring more happiness. Iacocca quickly reached the point in his life where, as he himself said, making money was easier than spending it.

To some extent, Iacocca once again was trapped by his own language. There is ample evidence that he saw himself as a corporate leader and industrial pathfinder, not just someone making money. But his language and way of conceptualizing himself and his work was drawn from the old corporate model of winners and losers, where winning was defined by how much money you made. He was engaged in a new transition but was using old language, which in turn limited his view and thus his reality. What we feel he needed in his retirement was a worthy goal and challenge that he found deserving of his abilities, interests, and status.

It is interesting that he never took very seriously the task of attempting to revise his life goals. Most people faced with the number and severity of crises that came through Iacocca's life would have done some extensive life revision. Instead his response to these periods (being fired at Ford, Mary's death, the challenging years at Chrysler) always seemed to be to work harder for the company. It was almost as if he felt the way you dealt with a crisis was either to get a new job or work harder at the one you had. This approach worked well in the world of work—but it was a failure in the area of retirement. Retirement is essentially a personal experience, not a corporate one. Iacocca seemed uncomfortable exploring new personal dimensions of himself. Even his retirement activities seemed to focus on corporate ventures rather than expanding his horizons in new and personally satisfying directions. If his words are to be believed, his retirement was not all that productive or satisfying. He was without the essential relationships he would like, drifting without a strong central purpose, and personally unfulfilled.

What Iacocca failed to do was to recognize that the transition to retirement should be an opportunity to rethink the entire second half of one's adult life. Life expectancy has changed dramatically during this century. A person today who retires at age 60 may have as many years left to live as they spent in their entire work career. In his book *Halftime*, Bob Buford discusses this concept of the second half of life. Buford argues that the key to a satisfactory second half is to move from *success* to *significance*.[64] During the career cycle, for men especially, many people are focused on earning money and achieving success. Later in life, satisfaction may depend far more on doing something that has personal meaning and significance. Buford believes that the years prior to retirement should be spent examining what activities we can engage in that will produce this sense of satisfaction and significance. He also argues that to be most effective, one should begin planning for the second half well before retirement, and should put at least parts of this plan into effect before one's primary career ends.

An important lesson we can learn from Iacocca is that the years before retirement are an ideal time to reevaluate our life goals. The best retirement plans are generated well before the retirement phase begins. And those retirement plans begin with a careful rethinking of our goals and priorities for this next stage of our life.

The Importance of Planning

Iacocca seems to have done little careful planning for his retirement. In part this may have been because his image of retirement was such a negative one. If you believe you are leaving something very important for something unimportant, you are inclined to believe it will just take care of itself. There is little evidence that Iacocca developed specific or detailed plans for what he wanted to do in his retirement. He did not seem to have engaged in thoughtful self-reflection about the kind of person he was, and the kinds of things that would be satisfying and rewarding to him as he entered the next stage of his life. In part this was because Iacocca did not see retirement as the major life transition that it is. If you see yourself as just "stopping work," rather than embarking on a new stage of life, you are less likely to see the importance of identifying new goals and new directions.

Looking back, after he had retired, Iacocca admitted that self-reflection in relation to planning for retirement was important, and that he himself had not planned well. "You can plan everything in life, and then the rest caves in on you because you haven't done enough thinking about who you are and what you should do with the rest of your life."[65]

This lack of planning and self-reflection is all the more interesting because, as a highly successful CEO of a huge organization, systematic thinking and strategic planning for the future were an integral part of Iacocca's corporate life. He emphasized planning throughout his corporate career. At the age of 36, when Iacocca became general manager of the

Ford Division, he developed a management system that he continued to use from then on. He asked his key people, "What are your objectives for the next ninety days? What are your plans, your priorities, your hopes? And how do you intend to go about achieving them?"[66] These would be great questions to ask yourself as you begin to contemplate retirement. But it doesn't seem that Iacocca took his own advice when it came to retirement.

Iacocca emphasized the importance of putting your plans in writing. "As I'd learned from (Robert) McNamara, the discipline of writing something down is the first step toward making it happen."[67] And he agreed that "putting your ideas on paper is usually the best way of thinking them through."[68]

Part of planning for retirement is knowing why you are retiring, but Iacocca's thoughts about his reasons for retiring seem vague and oversimplified. Like the reasons given by many people, the reasons Iacocca described were mostly negative. His thoughts did not seem to reflect careful thinking or detailed planning. They were more often about what he was stopping than about new things he was excited to do.

As we have seen, the outcome was that Iacocca's retirement, even in his own assessment, was a failure. One can't help but wonder whether his movement to the second half of life would have been satisfying if he had given it the same kind of thought and planning that he gave to decisions he made in his corporate world.

What can we learn from Iacocca's example? If you are the kind of person who needs a full and active life to be satisfied, planning for your retirement is important. The transition to this new phase of life should not be taken for granted, or just expected to take care of itself. It should not be perceived as just a cessation of work, but a transition to a new phase of life. Planning for this stage of life should include not just financial planning, but planning for the personal side of retirement as well. Some people will even find that a written plan can be extremely useful. You should review your goals, your priorities, and the activities that will be meaningful to you personally. You should consider the impact on your relationships. You should engage in careful and systematic self-reflection about the kind of person you are and the kinds of things that would be satisfying and rewarding to you as you enter the next stage of life. The transition to retirement is a major life change equivalent to a career choice, a career change, a marriage, or a major move to a new location. You should give it the kind of careful attention that you would give any other major life change.

Retiring Gradually

For some people a sudden and total cessation from work may not be the best idea. A gradual transition into retirement may be more desirable. It seems clear from an examination of Lee Iacocca's life that his work was very important to him, and to his sense of identity. His comments in *Fortune* magazine, where he stated how unhappy he was in his retirement, related mostly to "missing the action." He was one of those people for whom work was the central focus of his life. Had he been more self-aware and more in touch with his own needs, he might have designed a retirement where he continued to work on some vital project or area of concern on a limited basis. Instead, he stopped completely, and then found himself searching for ways to recreate some kind of a work life.

For many people who are like Iacocca, a sudden transition to complete retirement may not be a good idea. In today's society it is no longer necessary to assume, as Iacocca did, that retirement from one job means total cessation of work. What we can learn from Iacocca is that, prior to retirement from your primary career, it may be worth seriously examining meaningful new work possibilities. If a total work stoppage is not desirable, the planning for some continued professional involvement should be initiated well before retirement. This could involve a shift to part-time work in your existing job, a new part time job, or even a new full time occupation. What we should not do is simply assume, without thinking it through, that a sudden and complete cessation of work will be fully satisfying. This will be especially true for people who thrive on the challenge of their work.

The Three R's of Retirement

We believe that a good retirement requires attention to what we call the "Three R's of Retirement." These are one's responsibilities, relationships, and recreation. *Responsibilities* include what we perceive as our various duties, tasks and obligations in life. For those who are working, the primary activities in this category may relate to employment. But this is a bigger category than just work; it includes all those tasks that require attention in living a responsible life. *Relationships* encompass the satisfaction we get from interacting with those around us, including spouse, children, family, friends, colleagues, and social networks. *Recreation* includes all those non-work activities that give us pleasure, such as hobbies, sports, and entertainment. We don't think every person has to view each of these three areas as equally important, but we do think that each area should be thoughtfully examined by everyone planning retirement.

Iacocca seemed to thrive on his work responsibilities. His talk about relationships and recreation seems to pale next to the excitement of work. In fact if one examines the time line of his career, some of his most intense periods of work happened alongside periods of great significance in his relationships. In the five-year period starting from the time just after he left Ford, his wife had two heart attacks, a stroke, and complications from diabetes, which subsequently led to her death. Iacocca was aware of the negative effects of stress on diabetes, and later pointed out that each of Mary's heart attacks and her stroke followed a period of great stress at his job. But there is very little discussion of this in his books.

It is true that Iacocca states that family is important, and that he tried to reserve his weekends for his wife and family. He also encouraged his employees to use their vacation time. However, in his books, with the exception of relatively minor discussion of his family, and some comments about colleagues at Ford and Chrysler, there is not much to indicate that relationships were on a priority equal to his work. He seemed to think about his relationships less than his corporate existence, and understood them less well. At least on this dimension, his relationships were less successful than his corporate life.

Iacocca's books also say almost nothing about what he does for recreation and pleasure. One gets the strong feeling that this is not an accident: by far the most important thing in Iacocca's life was his work, above personal relationships and recreation. Iacocca does not seem to have thought through the balance of the "Three R's" of his life, and his transition to retirement does not seem to have made him happy.

It is important for a person to have a good perspective with respect to the "Three R's" of responsibilities, relationships, and recreation. A satisfactory retirement means thinking about all three of these areas and how important each is in your life. If a person focuses the majority of his or her energy in the work arena, it is especially difficult to have an effective transition to retirement when that arena no longer exists.

It is not easy to go into retirement and find your purpose once you get there. The message for us is that attending to each of the "Three R's" is important as we approach retirement. We need to think through all three of these areas, and give each of them a proper weighting as we try to balance their relative importance in our lives.

Just as this book is going to press, Iacocca has published a new book, *Where Have All The Leaders Gone?* It is a powerful, insightful, hard-hitting, common sense critique of American society and its leaders. Maybe we have underestimated Iacocca and been too harsh. He might have thought of his early retirement as a failure, but at the age of 82 he seems to have made a nice transition from success to significance.

LIFE AFTER WORK

4

Katharine Hepburn:
Taking Care

Retirement Can Be Different for Women

Women's retirements often differ from men's retirements. When men work, their work typically dominates their lives. In contrast, women who work often continue to pay intense attention to the needs of family and relationships. According to Frederic Hudson, who has spent a lifetime studying adult development, "there are dramatic differences between the styles and priorities of men and women during the adult life cycle."[1] Hudson argues that men invest highly in their careers in the early adult years, whereas women invest highly in caretaking roles — often in addition to their jobs and careers. Many studies have found that this difference continues throughout their adult lives: men tend to focus more on careers and success, while women focus on relationships.

This difference between men and women can produce profound differences in the way men and women experience retirement. The striking thing that makes women's retirement different is the central role relationships play in their lives. For women, the decision to retire, and the experience of retirement, is often critically affected by the needs and circumstances of those close to them—their spouse, their partner, their aging parents, and even their children.

One woman whose life illustrates this tension between career and relationships is Katharine Hepburn. While her life is unique in many ways, the Katharine Hepburn story has much to tell us.

Katharine Hepburn was a person well ahead of her time with respect to a woman's role. She was independent, iconoclastic, successful, and self-reliant. Arguably the most successful actress of the twentieth century, her career spanned more than 60 years. She received 12 Academy Award nominations for Best Actress and won 4 Academy Awards—more than any other actress in history. Most impressively, there was a span of 48 years between her first Academy Award and her last. She was widely regarded as one of the most independent, headstrong, self-sufficient women in America. But paradoxically, she decided to end her career because of her lifelong relationship with one man: the powerful, driven, outwardly confident but inwardly insecure, and self destructive, Spencer Tracy.

The Backstory

Early Years

By all accounts Katharine Hepburn did not have a traditional childhood. In almost every way her childhood was unique for the time in which she lived. Her father, Thomas Norval Hepburn, was the son of an Episcopalian minister; he studied medicine at Johns Hopkins University and later specialized in the treatment of venereal disease. He remained a role model for her throughout her life. Katharine Houghton Hepburn, her nontraditional mother, was from solid New England stock, but the product of a stormy and unconventional childhood. "Kit" Houghton, who became a force in the women's movement, encouraged her daughters in nontraditional thinking. Mrs. Hepburn exposed her children to political meetings and demonstrations on women's suffrage, birth control, and other liberal issues. Young Kate was enlisted to carry signs and hand out leaflets, later reflecting "I learned early what it is to be snubbed for a good cause. Snobbery has never worried me since."[2] The Hepburns had a significant circle of nontraditional friends including militant feminist Emmeline Pankhurst, anarchist Emma Goldman, and novelist Sinclair Lewis. Katharine Hepburn always described growing up in glowing terms: "I had the most wonderful childhood."[3]

Born on May 12, 1907 in Hartford, Connecticut, Katharine Houghton Hepburn was the second child in a family that included six children.[4] There were three boys and three girls in her family, and all the children were encouraged to participate in athletics. Katharine was something of a tomboy in the traditional sense, and had a strong admiration for her older brother Tom. She was good at figure skating, swimming, diving, golf and tennis. She also had inclinations towards sports that were very unusual for women, such as wrestling and the trapeze.

Not only did the Hepburns encourage her to excel in athletics, she was encouraged to believe that women were on a par with men. "I really was not brought up to feel that women were underdogs. I was totally unaware that we were the second-rate sex."[5] Called "Jimmy" by her friends and family, young Kate cut her hair short so it would not be a bother in sports and wrestling matches.

Katharine was about 13 when a dramatic change occurred in her life. She and her brother Tom were visiting a good friend of their mother's in New York. The two children were enjoying sightseeing and visiting when the visit turned somber. On Easter morning 1921, Katharine discovered the body of her beloved brother hanging in the attic bedroom. He had committed suicide by fashioning a rope and noose from torn sheets. After running to get help, Katharine rushed back to Tom and attempted to free him from the noose that was around his neck. Seventeen minutes later the doctor arrived from the local hospital and found Kate, sobbing, still holding her brother's stiff body off the floor to relieve the tension from the noose.[6] The suicide was a surprise and a mystery to all concerned. The headline in the *New York Times* echoed the sentiment: MYSTERY IN SUICIDE OF SURGEON'S SON.[7] The family tried to explain it as a childish prank gone wrong. Kate had a hand in fashioning and promoting this story. However, the circumstances surrounding the event suggest that the suicide was intentional.

Tom's death was hard on Kate, who became moody and withdrawn in her grief. Acting seemed one of the few things that interested her and she was encouraged in that direction. That same year Kate was removed from the public school system and home-schooled. Her tutoring was rigorous and by the age of 16 she was admitted to Bryn Mawr College. She lacked the social skill necessary to fit in well there, and often her encounters were awkward or strained. Most of the girls at Bryn Mawr were more at ease and better groomed than Kate.[8] She had trouble fitting in, and most of the people there did not understand her. The theater seemed to provide her with a way to be accepted and valued. She had several roles and some small successes in the college plays. She determined that what she wanted to do with her life was to become an actress.

Acting

Once she decided on an acting career, Katharine Hepburn embarked on this effort with remarkable energy and commitment. It was a choice of career that she knew would not sit well with her successful upper class parents. Her father detested actors, and she dreaded what his reactions would be when she told him she had chosen acting as a career.

Her first efforts to break into acting were not what she might have hoped for. She landed a part as understudy to the leading actress in a play to be brought to Broadway, and got the kind of break an aspiring actor dreams of. After a particularly passionate reading, she was given the lead role. But at the out-of-town performance before the Broadway opening, her rapid-fire delivery was almost impossible for the audience to understand, and the next day she was fired.[9]

In the meantime, she was being pursued by suitor Ludlow Ogden Smith, whom Kate had met when he was 28 and she was still in college. Luddy and his friend Jack Clark both were infatuated by Kate. Neither succeeded in seducing the attractive young Hepburn. However, she did strip off her clothes and pose for dozens of nude photographs on the living-room couch. "I posed with total confidence, as I rather fancied myself," recalled Kate, who placed the nude photos in a straw basket for anyone to see.[10]

During college, Kate seemed less interested in marriage than in her career. But when her career seemed to be going nowhere and she couldn't get a part, she made the youthful decision to quit the theater for good, marry the man who had pursued her so persistently, and become a housewife. On December 12, 1928, at age of 21, Katharine Hepburn became Mrs. Ogden Ludlow. Ludlow Ogden Smith changed his name to Ogden Ludlow so Kate's married name would not be Kate Smith, the name of a popular but corpulent singer of the time. The wedding took place in the Hepburn home in Hartford with Kate's eighty-three-old grandfather officiating.

Kate's decision to abandon acting lasted only two weeks. She told her husband she was desperately unhappy, she just *had* to act. And Luddy, who would do anything for her, agreed to support her efforts.[11]

Gradually, Kate began to have more success as a theater actress. There were ups and downs, and she was fired from more than one play before she "stood Broadway on its ear" with a performance that ultimately led to a contract in Hollywood.[12] Once in Hollywood, she had her share of roles in films that were flops, and her share of bad reviews, but also some remarkable success. She was in her mid twenties when she had a huge hit in *Morning Glory* and earned her first Academy Award.[13] During this climb toward fame as an actress, her personal life was equally erratic. In Hollywood, the now married Katharine Hepburn began an affair with her agent, Leland Hayward.[14] There were also rumors of a lesbian relationship with her constant companion, Laura Harding.[15] Her husband Luddy continued to hope that she would come to her senses and return to him. He did not formally seek a divorce until many years later, in 1942, when he sought to marry someone else. Kate and Luddy remained lifelong friends. After the death of his second wife, Kate helped care for Luddy through the illness that led to his death in 1979.[16]

Kate's wild and untamed ways continued. She began a tempestuous affair in 1936 with the wealthy adventurer, entrepreneur, and playboy Howard Hughes. This high-profile liaison between two headstrong, narcissistic and powerful individuals provided fodder for the press and gossip columns. Hughes was a daring aviator who held the cross country air speed record for many years. Once Kate flew Hughes' seaplane under a bridge in New York City, and they often skinny-dipped off its pontoons in Long Island Sound.[17] The energetic pair frequently flew cross country together. Hughes and Hepburn were alike in being "ruthless in pursuit of their own interests," according to Christopher Anderson, author of *An Affair to Remember.*[18] He quotes Cary Grant on the couple: "They were like two wild horses. Nobody was about to tame either one of them."[19]

There was much speculation about the possible marriage of these two fascinating figures. Newspapers predicted their impending marriage several times. But while there were several proposals from Hughes, Kate never really said yes, and finally she said no.

Kate had decided early on that it was impossible for her to pursue a normal family life and also a career—and she chose the career. She later reflected that "ambition beat love."[20] Hollywood reporter James Bacon said "she simply wasn't interested in being married." So while Hughes continued to pursue her and desperately tried to get her to say yes, in the end she told him she did not want to marry him—or anyone else—ever![21]

Hepburn's negative views toward marriage—for herself, at least—remained consistent throughout her life. Later, discussing why she never cared about being married to her longtime lover Spencer Tracy, she noted that she just wasn't suited for marriage. She said she thought an actor should never marry—even another actor. She felt actors were too involved with themselves, too self-possessed. She also thought the work was too demanding to give the necessary time and attention to a family and children. Far from disparaging the role of housewife and mother, Hepburn felt it was one of the most important jobs in the world—but only if a person really wanted to do it, and she didn't. "I did not want to be married, I just wanted to be myself…Being a housewife and a mother … didn't interest me, so I didn't do it."[22]

Hepburn Meets Tracy

Throughout her life, Katharine Hepburn intimidated most of the men she came in contact with. She was described by a screenwriter she worked with as "terrifying" and "a tornado."[23] Even her directors, such as Elia Kazan, were to say things such as "I was scared of Kate. I was overpowered by her."[24] She was fiercely independent, even dominant and arrogant. Even her habits were uniquely hers. She refused ever to wear dresses except on the set, preferring men's slacks, and was often seen lounging with her feet up higher than her head. She claimed to bathe five times a day. She loved to take icy swims in Long Island Sound, a habit she continued into her eighties, claiming that bitter medicine is good for you.[25]

One man not intimidated by Kate was Spencer Tracy. The two had not yet met when Kate became convinced she wanted to work with Tracy as an actor in a movie she was planning called *Woman of the Year*. When the producer Joe Mankiewicz introduced them, she had on high heel shoes that made her taller than Tracy. She apologized, and said that in the movie she'd be careful what she wore. "Don't worry, Kate," said Mankiewicz. "He'll cut you down to size."[26] It was 1941. She was 34 years old and he was 41. Their lives would remain deeply intertwined until his death 26 years later.

The only thing Kate knew about Tracy when they met was the same thing everyone in Hollywood knew. He was a superb actor who had already won two Academy Awards for Best Actor. He also had a huge drinking problem, one that frequently threatened his work and, eventually, his life.

Spencer Tracy was as complex an individual as Katharine Hepburn, but they were very different. Growing up poor in downtown Milwaukee, he was known early for his quick temper and explosive personality. A tough street kid who got into fights at the slightest provocation, Tracy was drawn early to the stage. By the time he met Kate he was known as a superb actor, greatly admired by his peers and the public alike.

The great actors of that period all admired Tracy's acting skills. James Cagney described him as the best actor he'd ever known.[27] Humphrey Bogart said "as far as actors go . . . I'd say Spence is the best by far."[28] Clark Gable said "There's nobody in this business who can touch him."[29] Even the great Laurence Olivier said he "learned more about acting from watching Tracy than any other way."[30] The public also praised his abilities. *Time* magazine called him "cinema's No. 1 actor's actor,"[31] and the *New York Times* hailed one performance as "perfection itself."[32] Kate had the same reaction. Years before she met him, she saw him in a film role she described as "the best goddamned performance I've ever seen," and "so remarkable that it is as total as birth or death."[33]

Fellow actors described him as a wonderfully natural actor. He was the exact opposite of Kate in this respect. Kate labored over every scene and studied every part in great detail, but he just "read the lines" and *became* the person he was acting in a way that amazed his fellow actors. Spencer would blow up at Kate for laboring over a scene and tell her to just *do* it.

But beneath Tracy's superb acting skills was a complex and disturbed personality. Even after an intimate relation of 25 years, Kate was to say after Tracy's death that she never completely understood him. He permanently separated from his wife after the first few years of marriage, yet he remained married to her and concerned for her welfare for all of his life. He was a noted womanizer, and made no secret of his affairs with such famous stars as Loretta Young, Myrna Loy, Joan Crawford, and Ingrid Bergman.[34] But despite the surface bluster and self-confidence, underneath he was filled with self-doubt. He had lifelong guilt over the fact that his first son was born deaf. He had chronic insomnia and a terrible fear of flying. He was a hypochondriac and suffered anxiety attacks.[35] Film directors were well aware of his bouts of insecurity, and his tendency to suddenly get cold feet and want to back out of almost every movie, just as filming was about to begin. He had a lifelong struggle with alcohol that at times threatened to ruin his career, and eventually did ruin his health. He could be friendly and outgoing, but at other times he was tactless, rude, and even mean.[36] Those close to him described him as driven by personal demons. Bette Davis recalled him as "a very deeply troubled, unhappy man. Full of doubt and rage."[37]

This was the man to whom Katharine Hepburn was so powerfully drawn. From the moment Kate and Spencer began work on their first film together, everyone around them could see that the spark of passion between them was more than just a screen role. "I knew right away that I found him irresistible. Just exactly that—irresistible!"[38] She was strangely attracted to this man who was so powerful and dominant, and yet in some ways so needy. Christopher Anderson theorized that Tracy somewhat resembled her father, and perhaps he served in a way as both a father and a child surrogate to Kate.[39]

Kate's relation with Tracy seemed to contradict every other aspect of her life. The woman who was so strong and even domineering in every other arena seemed to become a subservient and adoring slave in Spencer's presence. Even when he treated her badly, she always supported him and defended him. Her friends were dumbfounded that this aggressive and hard-driving woman would curl up at Spencer's feet, gazing up at him as he stroked her hair lovingly. While fierce, competent, accomplished and competitive in her own right, she seemed totally devoted to the hard drinking, drug taking, anxiety ridden hypochondriac that was the real life Spencer Tracy.

This unusual relationship would continue for a quarter century. They made many films together, and many more apart from each other. For months at a time he would be filming in Hollywood while she was busy acting in a play in New York, or off filming on location somewhere else, shooting scenes for *The African Queen* in the Congo, or working on other films in Europe. At other times she would be in Hollywood while he filmed abroad. Yet they always got back together. Most often it was Kate who flew to be by Tracy's side. Sometimes it was to be with him as he recuperated from another drinking binge. Sometimes it was to offer support when it seemed like he might fall off the wagon. Sometimes they just seemed to be the perfect romantic couple, walking hand in hand along the shore.

Long before Katharine Hepburn entered what was seen as her retirement from her film and acting career, it was obvious to several people close to her that she had begun to put the needs of Spencer Tracy before her own career. It was hard to believe, but this dynamic, head-strong, successful, progressive woman, seemed to make every career choice in deference to Tracy.

Her devotion to him was unshakable. When his health became uncertain, she began to structure her entire career around his needs. She turned down numerous roles in order to be near him, especially at times when it seemed he might be at risk for another bout of drinking. At times she seemed almost to be his slave—she picked him up at his hotel, drove him to the studio, brewed coffee for him on the set, fed him lunch, cooked him dinner, straightened his tie, and screened his phone calls.

She was very conscious that she had chosen to make him the focus of her life. "He was there—I was his. I wanted him to be happy, safe, and comfortable. I liked to wait on him—listen to him—feed him—talk to him—work for him."[40] She cared for him with loving affection and without regret.

This is all the more unbelievable because everyone who knew her said what a tough character she was. She took no guff and showed no quarter to anyone—except Spencer Tracy. "Looking back, I was blinded from the moment I met him" she once remarked.[41] Unlike the affairs with Leland Hayward and Howard Hughes, she seemed to find a deep purpose and meaning in helping Tracy. An actor friend said that "Those other fellows didn't really need her, and she knew it. . . Just the fact that someone needs you can be a powerful aphrodisiac."[42] But simplistic explanations like that don't do justice to this enormously complex relationship.

She knew that in making Tracy her priority she was, for the first time in her life, putting her career in second place. It was as large a commitment as one could make. Her commitment to Tracy was unqualified. As one biographer concluded:

> From 1942 on, every professional decision Kate made — every stage and movie role she accepted or refused — was arrived at on the basis of how it affected Spencer. Over the next eight years she starred in only ten films, six of them with Tracy.[43]

She seemed unaffected by how gruffly he treated her. He might react to a deeply felt comment she made with a dismissive "who the hell asked you?" But beneath his roughness—sometimes bordering on meanness—he had enormous respect for her and would listen to her in a way he listened to no one else.

Hepburn seemed to be fully aware of the task she had taken on. She once remarked that, "If you are going to help anybody who is in trouble, this is not a two-hour-a-day job. It is a twenty-four-hour-a-day job. You won't do anything else if you decide that you are going to resurrect and rearrange a human being."[44] By all accounts she had taken on a large task. It was to be a long a wild ride with Tracy. The bouts of drinking and debauchery, followed by periods of sensitive normalcy (which seemed to prove to her that he was redeemable), provided her with a challenge that she seemed to relish.

Tracy himself ran hot and cold with respect to actually encouraging her to be involved in his life. At times she would find him drunk in a bar, take him home, clean him up, only to have him berate her in a drunken rage and exile her from his hotel room. She was not above sleeping in the hall outside his room in case he needed additional care. It was an incredible contradiction to everything else she stood for that this rich, famous, powerful woman was willing to sleep outside his door like a faithful cocker spaniel, waiting for him to pass through his mean drunken state and return to treating her with some civility. Yet she seemed to harbor no feelings of regret or resentment about any of this.

Both of them were committed to keeping their relationship out of the public eye. He no longer lived with his wife, but he was determined to keep his relationship with Hepburn a private one. Spencer and Kate never lived in the same house, and never stayed in the same hotel. In certain ways she even gave up some of her dignity for him. When they traveled together, night after night, she would walk to his hotel from her own, sneaking up a back stairway, or riding up a service elevator, and leaving later by the same route. The press joined in a silent conspiracy to avoid the probing gossip that followed so many other famous stars.

Katharine Hepburn's almost total restructuring of her life to meet Tracy's needs was striking in someone who was otherwise independent, self-assured and even domineering. Wherever she worked she was respected, admired and even feared. She was not afraid to stand up to anyone. She was always on time for rehearsal, and willing to speak sharply to anyone who was late, no matter how famous they were. During the filming of *Suddenly Last Summer*, when co-star Elizabeth Taylor was late and kept them waiting on the set, she would not put up with it—*nobody* kept Katharine Hepburn waiting. Irritated with the irresponsibility of her co-stars on that film, Hepburn began to compensate by taking over part of the directing herself. Soon Hepburn and the famous director Joseph Mankiewicz were screaming at each other, and at one point it got so bad that Mankiewicz threatened to close down the production if she didn't stop interfering. She was absolutely fearless in standing up for anything she believed in.

It is a full conundrum that Katharine Hepburn, who was so committed to professionalism and expertise in every detail of her films, and her life, would have tolerated a personal companion with so many weaknesses and such major life flaws as Spencer Tracy. He was the one true exception to everything she seemed to stand for. For the rest of the world, anything less than competent perfection would encounter her wrath. Where Tracy was concerned, Kate made enormous allowances.

When Tracy was making a film, Kate would often accompany him on the set. She would attend to his needs, make sure he took his pills, and bring him water and food when he needed it. She seemed a combination of a hovering mother hen and an enchanted admirer. When a scene was complete, she would rush forward and say "wasn't he *terrific?*" before anyone else could comment. Kate ardently defended Tracy against any criticism. The director Joseph Mankiewicz said that "Kate adored Spencer, worshiped him. When she was around him, she sometimes did behave like some awestruck kid. But she enjoyed it."[45] The director Elia Kazan said "The cause Hepburn believed in was Tracy.... She truly adored him."[46] And she herself said later, "People are shocked that I gave up so much for a man. But you have to understand it gave *me* pleasure to make him happy, to ease his agony."[47]

Kate stuck by Spencer through bouts of drinking and a spats of terrible temper that would have driven away most women.

But two such powerful giants could not always get along. "We had plenty of arguments," Kate said. "That goes with the territory when two reasonably intelligent, stubborn people care about each other."[48] But they always made up. George Cukor, one of their best friends, said "they could bicker and argue and say dreadful things to one another. But they always came out of it laughing and hugging, like teenagers."[49]

Spencer Tracy had a dark side that came out unpredictably. He could be generous one minute, and vicious the next. While working on the film *The Mountain* in the Swiss Alps, one scene required a cable-car trip to the top of the mountain. Tracy's co-star, the young Robert Wagner, was frightened of the ride. Tracy, despite his own fear of flying and heights, generously offered to accompany Wagner even though he wasn't required for that scene. The ride turned into a nightmare. Halfway up the mountain in the enclosed cable car, some of the wheels slipped off the cable, making the car drop several feet and swing back and forth so violently that the windshield shattered. All the passengers on board feared they were about to die. They were rescued after a long complicated ordeal. Everyone was shaken by the experience, and Tracy himself had to be held up as he staggered out of the cable car.

That night Tracy went to the hotel bar and drank heavily. His mood shifted from talkative and charming to violent. Suddenly and with no apparent provocation, Tracy glared at a waiter approaching with a tray of drinks. Without warning, he picked up his empty glass and threw it at the waiter's face. Robert Wagner reacted quickly and raised his hand to block the glass. The glass shattered in Wagner's hand and cut him badly. As people attended to Wagner, Tracy was carted off to his room to sleep it off.

In the morning Tracy claimed to remember none of the incident. It was a strange and bizarre series of events made even more eerie by Tracy's dark side. Wagner, still overcome with the horror of the cable car incident, forgave his friend, but others were deeply concerned. When Kate learned of Tracy's violent outburst she sent her personal secretary to the scene to be of help. Even Tracy's brother Carroll arrived a few days later to help out. There were no more incidents during the filming but Tracy got drunk again at the farewell party before the trip home. On the drive to the airport he began tossing beer bottles out the car window. On the return flight home Tracy again drank himself into a stupor. By the time he arrived in Los Angeles he was so drunk the pilot of the plane taxied to a closed off area where he was carried to a waiting car and driven to his cottage on the Cukor estate. He continued to drink. With Kate out of town for a few days Tracy went club crawling and drinking with *Mountain* co-star Anna Kashfi. The two disappeared for two weeks before he returned to the Cukor cottage. [50]

It is hard to understand why Kate was so committed to Spencer, but she was. Katharine Hepburn was powerfully attracted to Spencer Tracy from the moment they met. She loved him for their entire 27 years together and her love was unwavering and nonjudgmental. She loved him despite—and perhaps in part because of—the fact that he was a deeply troubled man.

> I love you. What does this mean? . . . Love has nothing to do with what you are expecting to get—only with what you are expecting to give—which is everything. . . . It really implies total devotion. . . . I loved Spencer Tracy. He and his interests and his demands came first. This was not easy for me because I was definitely a *me, me, me*, person. It was a unique feeling that I had for [Tracy]. I would have done anything for him. . . . We ate what he liked. We did what he liked. We lived a life which he liked. . . . I found him irresistible. Just exactly that. [51]

Her love was constant even though she knew he was a tortured man. She wrote about it later. "[At night] you would turn and turn and turn and sigh . . . never at peace . . . tortured by some sort of guilt, some terrible misery. Was it that you couldn't stand yourself?"[52]

She never tried to change him. Perhaps aware that it would do no good, she never tried to get him to stop drinking. She stood by him in other ways, as well. During their many times apart, Tracy was not above turning to other women. He had brief affairs with at least two other famous actresses, Gene Tierney and Grace Kelly, while he was involved with Kate.[53]

None of this seemed to make much difference to the special relationship he had with Katharine Hepburn.

There were many times when Hepburn had long battles trying to terminate stage and film commitments so she could be back with him during times when she felt he needed her. Arguably, her career languished from 1942 to 1951 then enjoyed a surge with five Academy Award nominations between 1951 and 1962. During that time Tracy continued to slide steadily down hill in his personal life. In 1955 he was actually fired from the film *Tribute to a Bad Man*, ending his twenty year career at MGM. The experience was devastating to Tracy and confirmed Hepburn's belief that she might be the only person who could coax Tracy back to stability. Tracy was even more confused, weak and self-destructive after the firing. There were occasional periods of stability, but the overall downward slide continued. Each time Hepburn would attempt to attend to her own career it seemed to be matched by another downward step on Tracy's part. By 1962 Tracy was at the bottom.

In the ten-year period prior to 1959 Spencer Tracy had announced his retirement at least a dozen times. Whenever he completed a film, he vowed it would be his last. No one took him seriously until *The Last Hurrah*. He was not yet sixty, but it was clear to everyone that Tracy was a very, very, sick man. All the old medical problems were still there, and the breathing difficulties were now officially diagnosed as emphysema. "He feared every breath might be his last. His liver, bladder and kidneys no longer functioned properly. He had an enlarged prostate. He suffered from high blood pressure. He was terrified that years of drink were destroying his memory."[54] In his book, *An Affair to Remember*, Anderson concludes, "It was equally clear that if Tracy retired, his lover/nurse/best friend/

soul-mate would follow him into the sunset. She would always, it was understood, put his interests before hers."[55]

Almost always with the care and encouragement of Hepburn, Tracy did some of his best work in the '50s. There is general agreement that without Kate to guide him, nurse him, care for him, and rehabilitate him from his debauchery this would never have been possible. Whenever she was away from him or he was away from her he seemed to take another step down. Together Tracy and Ernest Hemingway destroyed a bar in Havana (Tracy was there doing research for *Old Man and the Sea*), and on the set of *The Last Hurrah* Tracy had become so weak he had to take naps and long afternoon filming sessions were out of the question. The punishing life style took its toll. By 1962 he was weak and debilitated. He felt he was unable to work. But Kate felt that work would be good for him. She felt it might keep him from worry and from the idleness that would lead to bouts of drinking. She kept pushing to keep him occupied. But the parts he could manage were increasingly smaller.

"Retirement"

In 1962 Tracy's condition became so compelling that Kate turned her full attention to caring for him. Even though she was in great demand, she stopped accepting roles and offers. She did this with the full knowledge that it might mean the end of her career. She knew there were only a limited number of roles for an actress in her mid fifties. She also knew that acting was a kind of career where obscurity is death. Hepburn herself said, "In this business it's hard to make what people call a comeback . . . in this business people just forget you."[56] At the peak of her career, just after winning an Academy Award, she gave it all up and decided to walk away knowing that she might never be able to come back.

She turned her primary energy to caring for Spencer Tracy and trying to nurse him back to health. It was a big job. In 1963 Tracy went on a drunk with James Bacon that was his last major bender, but his health already had been damaged beyond repair. In July of that year he landed in the hospital gasping for air and slipped into unconsciousness. Tracy had pulmonary edema (fluid in the lung tissue). In August he was back in the hospital. These incidents seemed pivotal in persuading Kate to retire from her career and devote herself fully and completely to helping Tracy.[57] It was a courageous and selfless choice. It was also a tremendous change from the younger Katharine Hepburn who let several good relationships molder because she said her career came first.

In the spring of 1964 Tracy had made something of a recovery, but was still too weak and ill to follow through on several parts he wanted to play. At times he needed oxygen for his failing heart, which Kate helped administer. In an interview he said he was like a prize fighter who felt good but couldn't make the weight. In truth, he was quite ill and not up to the task of work.

A review of Katharine Hepburn's film and stage credits will document that she had indeed "retired" to care for Spencer Tracy. [58] There is no body of work listed for the years from 1962, (when she won an Academy Award nomination for *Long Day's Journey into Night*) until 1967. She simply stopped working to care for Tracy — and risked being forgotten. It was a dramatic and major life decision.

Kate not only gave up her career, but she also endured a major change in her life style in order to be with Tracy. Their life styles were very different, but she mostly deferred to his. Tracy led a Spartan existence. He lived in a little carriage house on George Cukor's estate that had minimal creature comforts. The bedroom had little in it beyond an oak chest and a bed. Tracy didn't want to own anything that he couldn't fit into a suitcase. In contrast, Kate had enjoyed her life of privilege and comfort, and had lived in a home with abundant space surrounded by personal effects. She loved a house filled with special things that were meaningful to her, and was very attached to her possessions. "I like nothing better than to buy a house and fill it with all the things I cherish . . . all those silly and wonderful things that make a house a heartwarming experience to return to."[59] She left all of that to be with Tracy and accept his almost neurotic need for minimal living.

The years caring for the aging and ill Tracy were certainly difficult, but Kate never complained or seemed to mind. All Kate's energy was focused on what she thought would be good for him. Kate encouraged many things to help the healing process — preparing special meals, walks, flying kites, painting, and interesting evenings with friends. It was all designed to help the sometimes morose Tracy to have a fuller life.

She tried to divert him from his troubles. She brought him books to read, engaged him in passionate, good-natured literary discussions, and borrowed new movies for private screenings so he could keep up with his colleagues' work. Somehow she managed to do everything without ever making him feel like an invalid.[60]

But all this seemed to work only marginally well. Tracy's health continued to deteriorate and it became increasingly clear that his situation was very serious. Lurking in the background was the unstated fear that his days were numbered. At some point it became apparent that he was not improving and decisions had to be made about whether he would ever work again. Kate clung to the hope that work would be therapeutic despite the risk that it could hasten his end. Work might give him something else to think about besides his continuing physical decline.

In dialogue with Hepburn, Tracy began to warm to the idea of making one last film. Realizing he might not have long to live, part of his motivation may have been that he wanted to give Kate a vehicle to restart her career after years of caring for him. Late in 1966 Stanley Kramer approached the two of them with the idea for a new movie dealing with the controversial topic of race. Tracy had worked with Kramer before and liked him. Tracy knew he was declining rapidly and might die before the film was finished. Because Tracy was uninsurable due to his poor health, Kramer and Hepburn contrived a plan to make their entire salaries for the film available to cover the cost of re-shooting if Tracy died during the film shoot. Sidney Poitier and Katharine Houghton (Hepburn's niece) signed on, and the project was under way.

It is unclear what Tracy's motivation was to make one last film. The reasons were probably complex, but part of his motivation may have been to do it for Kate. He realized his powerful box office draw, and also realized the exponential power of the Tracy/Hepburn combination. It is possible that he was intent on doing this last film as a way of re-establishing Kate's career, knowing she would want to return to acting when he was gone. The plan, if that is a fair characterization, was a good one. Both he and Hepburn were nominated for Academy

Awards. She won the award for best actress, setting her off again on a thriving film career.

Guess Who's Coming to Dinner would be the last Tracy/ Hepburn film, and as usual Tracy would get top billing. When it was suggested by friends that the billing be reversed this once, as a way of thanking Hepburn for her support of him all these years, Tracy's response was true to form: "This is a movie, chowderhead, not a lifeboat."[61] It was typical of their relationship. Stanley Kramer observed first-hand how their partnership worked:

> Tracy would tell his beloved costar, "Just do what the director guy tells you, will yah?" and she'd reply, humbly, "all right." She'd take nothing from anybody else, from him everything.[62]

A few weeks before the filming began Tracy suffered a severe emphysema attack and collapsed. There were fears he would not make it to the end of the filming. On the first day of filming Sidney Poitier became quite emotional, as did everyone else on the set. They all knew they were watching a great actor, and they knew this would be the last picture Tracy would ever make.

The entire shooting schedule was structured to accommodate Spencer and his flagging energy. His shots were done between 9:00 AM and noon, and he no longer had the stamina to read the lines for the other actors' close-ups—not even Kate's. In several scenes where she is supposed to be talking to Spencer she was forced to deliver her lines to blank space. Even Kramer had to rely on Kate for hourly bulletins on Spencer's physical state.

Tracy was like a different person working on this film. No longer the raging drunk, he fought to keep his energy up, and cooperated in every way with the director. He was grateful for the concessions being made on his behalf, and exhibited true warmth towards the cast and the crew.

Kate was another matter. As always, she remained her obstreperous, forceful self. In addition to taking care of Spencer, she meddled in everything from the direction, to costumes, lighting, set design and make-up. Kramer said she had opinions about *everything*. He had never seen anything quite like it. One got the feeling that this was the way she always was, but now it was especially important. This was to be their last film and she wanted it to be particularly good.

It was a race to the end. As the shooting approached its final week, Tracy took Kramer aside and told him that he had been looking at the script and that if he died on his way home that day Kramer still had enough to release the picture.[63] They were racing time and everyone knew it.

In the film's emotional climax Christina Drayton (Kate) looks on, her eyes welling with tears, as Matt Drayton (Spencer) finally tells the parents of their daughter's black fiancé that "in the final analysis it doesn't matter what we think. The only thing that matters is what they feel, and how much they feel for each other. And if it's half of what we felt . . . that's everything."

Spencer was talking about Kate, about their love for each other, Kramer recalled of that moment. He was paying tribute to her before millions of people and saying good-bye. There wasn't a dry eye in the place.[64]

Tracy's Death

Two weeks after that final emotional scene, Spencer Tracy died of a heart attack. The events surrounding the end of Tracy and Hepburn's relationship were as unconventional as the relationship itself.[65] Public accounts of Tracy's death distorted the true story. Kate was with Tracy at the time of his death, but the adoring public would not find that out until decades later.

Tracy was increasingly incapacitated after the filming of *Guess Who's Coming to Dinner*, and in the days that followed it became apparent that the experience of making the film was not restorative to Tracy but had taken a medical toll. Both Tracy and Hepburn knew that Tracy was living out his last days. Kate would sit by his bed and talk with Tracy for hours. She cared for him, brought him his meals, and did everything she could to make him comfortable.

On June 10, 1967 Katharine Hepburn and Spencer Tracy talked late into the night, he propped up in bed and she lying on the carpet, head on a pillow near his bed. Finally Tracy tired and fell asleep, and Kate moved to her room. After several hours of sleep, Tracy made his way into the kitchen to make himself a cup of tea. It was there that he suffered a massive heart attack that ended his life. Kate heard him fall and the teacup smash on the kitchen floor. When she reached his side he was dead.

Kate's first reaction was to remove all evidence of their romantic relationship before Tracy's wife Louise arrived on the scene Kate called her friend and secretary Phyllis Wilbourn to come to the cottage and help her. They called the doctor. Then they got the housekeeper and gardener from next door, who helped Kate slide the body onto a small carpet, move it to the bedroom, and place it gently on the bed. Then Phyllis and the two women began to strip the small cottage of any evidence that Katharine Hepburn had ever been there. Clothes were taken from closets, dresser drawers were emptied, bathroom cabinet shelves were stripped, and all personal effects of Kate's were removed and loaded into Tracy's black Thunderbird.

But once the car was filled with all her belongings Kate had a change of heart. She realized that she did not in fact want to erase the footprints of her 27 years with Tracy, nor completely deny the existence of the relationship itself. Kate began to feel that now that Tracy was dead some of the rules had changed, and some other things that mattered when he was alive now ceased to matter. The need to conceal the relationship to the general public was in play but within her closer circles of friends and relationships Kate was beginning to feel less of a need for the charade. It is also reasonable to conclude that in her grief Kate longed for some "ownership" of the relationship that she had so dedicated herself to over the past 27 years. She seemed less willing, as the weight and gravity of Tracy's death began to sink in, to deny the relationship or its significance.

Another flurry of activity followed. Back went all the clothes, bathroom items, mementos, and personal effects. It was a nonverbal statement that Kate now wanted to lay some claim to the relationship, at least in private circles. Kate described her own confusion in her autobiography:

> We moved all my stuff—clothes, personal stuff—out into [the] car. Then I thought—God—Kath—what are you doing—you've lived with the man for almost thirty years. This is your home. Isn't it? It is part of you. These walls—this roof—this spot on the earth. I carried everything back into the house. You can't deny your life of thirty years.[66]

The awkwardness continued over the next hours and days. There was Kate, the committed partner of almost thirty years, and Louise, no longer his central companion but still legally his wife and still in possession of the role of wife. Reports that were given to the press left out Kate's role entirely and even described her as arriving on the scene only after the grieving widow, Louise, had begun making funeral arrangements.

It was awkward when Kate was the one who served bacon, eggs and toast to the arriving friends, and even to Louise herself. It was awkward for Kate to watch Louise make her way down the hallway of the cottage to be alone with the body in the bedroom. It was awkward when Kate picked out the burial suit only to have Louise object and say she should be the one to choose the suit. It was awkward when Kate visited the funeral home alone each day after everyone had gone, to sit beside the coffin. It was awkward when close friends paid their formal respects to Louise at the funeral home, and then made a separate trip to Tracy's cottage to offer comfort to Kate as Tracy's true partner.

Kate decided not to go to the funeral to avoid embarrassing Louise and the family. That morning, Kate and Phyllis took a final drive to the funeral home and seeing no one there they went in. Preparations were underway for the trip to the church. The two women asked if they could help load the coffin into the back of the hearse. Then they pulled their car behind the cortege and silently followed it toward the church. A block before the church they turned away and drove home. The greatest actress in the world did not want to act the part of being no more to Tracy than a good friend.

After the body was buried at Forest Lawn Cemetery, those who were closest to Spencer Tracy went directly to his cottage on the Cukor's estate to pay their respects to the person they knew was most significant to Tracy — Katharine Hepburn. It was obvious to everyone who visited the cottage that day how hard a blow Tracy's death had been for Kate. She was devastated and completely numb. Even though the death of Tracy was somewhat expected, it was still a shock of massive proportion.

The film *Guess Who's Coming to Dinner* was a blockbuster and won both Kate and Spencer Academy Award nominations. She won. He did not. She is rumored to have remarked: "It's OK. I'm sure mine is for the two of us."[67]

Only the Hollywood insiders knew about the 27 year relationship that was even more powerful than the one on screen. With the primary love of her life gone, Kate seemed off balance for a time. The days she had filled with caring for him were now empty. To fill the void Kate returned to the second love of her life — acting.

Kate's return to acting was motivated in part by her grief. She turned to work to keep her mind off her pain, "I don't want to think at all for two years," she said. "I'm going to work hard."[68] She returned to work and continued to be productive. Her self inflicted absence might have ended the career of someone of lesser character and talent. Her return was particularly impressive in field where there are a wealth of good actresses fighting for a few good roles, and in an industry where it is easy to be quickly forgotten — especially if you are a female over 50.

Her return to work was enormously successful. Not only did she receive an Academy Award at the age of 57 for her work with Tracy in *Guess Who's Coming to Dinner*, but the following year she received her third Academy Award for

A Lion in Winter. She continued and energetic involvement in film and stage. In 1981 she received her fourth Academy Award for her work in **On Golden Pond,** sharing the spotlight with her co-star Henry Fonda, who also won an Academy Award for best actor. Kate was 71 years old and an astonishing 48 years had passed between her first and fourth Academy Awards. Her acting career continued to the age of 79. She had appeared in 42 films, more than 35 theater productions, eight radio productions, and four television productions. In her later years she published two best selling volumes of memoirs. In addition to her four Academy Awards, she also received a total of 12 Academy Award nominations. No other actress has compiled such an impressive list of accomplishments. A large portion of these achievements occurred after her return from her self-imposed retirement.

What the Katharine Hepburn Story Tells Us

Retirement May Be Harder for Women

There are many ways in which the retirement experience of women may be different from that of men. Traditionally, careers have been less central in women's lives, and this is still true to some extent today. Women often feel the burden of balancing career and family more keenly than men. Women of retirement age today usually feel more responsible for the care of the children, the family, even the parents, than do the men around them. Surprisingly often, as a husband's parents grow older, it is the wife who visits them in the nursing home and worries about their needs, while their own son seems more than willing to let this burden pass to his wife. This tension between family and career can be felt throughout a woman's life. It is especially clear in the early child-rearing years, but can continue beyond that. For many women the kind of job they hold, their ability to relocate for job advancement, the hours they can put in, and numerous other job-related decisions are second to the needs of their family far more than is typical for men.

This continues to be true when it comes to retirement. For many women, more than men, the retirement decision is driven by the needs of their spouse or other family obligations. Women more often than men report that the timing of their retirement depended on when their husband might retire, or on their husband's health, or on the needs of their parents, or even the needs of their husband's parents. We believe this often makes retirement more complex and difficult for women.

117

For women entering retirement, more than for men, there may be a wider variety of complex factors surrounding retirement that make it especially difficult. The sections below identify and discuss some of those factors.

Retirement Based on a Partner's Health Is Difficult

When Katharine Hepburn decided to stop work at the height of her career, her decision was based totally on her relationship with Spencer Tracy and on the state of his declining health. This kind of retirement, based on the health of someone close to you—whether it is a spouse, partner, aging parent, other family member, or even a child—has special challenges. It can produce an extraordinary convergence of problems, each difficult in its own right, but even more difficult when several of them occur in combination. Katharine Hepburn is a striking example that even women with enormous power and influence can feel the strain of this challenge. Like Katharine Hepburn, many women face this challenge without complaining and cope with it impressively well.

Women tend to focus on relationships more than men. It has been argued that for women, relationships, not career, are their highest priority, and this was certainly true for Katharine Hepburn. Women in our society also are more likely to adopt—or be assigned—the caretaker role. For many women the retirement decision is almost wholly determined by the health of someone close to them.

Research confirms this conclusion. Virginia Richardson is a retirement counselor who noted that women "are typically the ones who care for ill husbands and older parents, including mothers-in-law and fathers-in-law."[69] Richardson cites research showing that 72 percent of all caregivers are women. She notes that 29 percent of all caregivers are daughters and many of them stopped working to give care. She concludes that, "Many working women retire involuntarily, against their wishes, to care for ailing spouses or parents."[70] Joel Savishinsky, author of *Breaking the Watch: The Meanings of Retirement in America*, makes the same point: "More people are now entering retirement with responsibilities for some elder. Seventy five percent of America's care givers are women and 20 percent of them are 65 and older. Females are more likely than males to retire because of care-giving responsibilities."[71]

Whether it is a woman or a man who stops working to care for someone close to them, having to retire in this way is extremely demanding. In an extreme or "worst case" scenario this situation produces a powerful convergence of potentially stressful events. Even though one would hope that few people would experience all of these events together, they are sufficiently common that anyone who retires to care for someone else may encounter several of these stresses:

- Your retirement may be involuntary and unplanned.
- You may have to give up your career prematurely, at time when it might be in full bloom.
- All your work and professional connections may have to be abandoned to care for your ill spouse.
- Caring for a seriously ill spouse may be one of the most difficult physical and emotional burdens you have to face.
- You may suffer a loss of income and financial well being, as a result of possibly losing two incomes — perhaps at the same time, and unexpectedly. Savings may also be

depleted by the illness, or the ultimate ending of one retirement income.

• If your spouse dies, you may be plunged into a major process of grief and reconstruction.

Retirement May Be Involuntary and Unexpected

When you retire largely to take care of an ailing spouse, your retirement is, in a sense, involuntary. In many ways it is like a forced retirement from a company that has downsized: it comes earlier than you had wanted; it is not what you had anticipated; it is not what you built your life plans around. It can mean interrupting a career in full flow, a sudden and unanticipated change in your definition of yourself. For all of these reasons, involuntary retirement is far more difficult than voluntary retirement. Research supports this: "Involuntary retirees have more problems adjusting to retirement and have higher rates of depression, lower morale, less life satisfaction, and unhappier retirement than do voluntary retirees."[72]

Such a retirement decision is usually unexpected. This means that some of the additional losses—the familiar social networks and the daily structure associated with the job—have come without warning, leaving the retiree disoriented and off balance. One research study found that "nearly 70 percent of the persons who retired as planned were content in their retirement, compared with less than 20 percent of those who retired unexpectedly because of poor health or loss of job."[73]

In addition to being involuntary and unexpected, a retirement due to health reasons may also be a sudden one. If the health changes occur suddenly, it means there are very major life changes that may have to be made in a short period of time. An enormous number of practical concerns must be dealt with, from finances to housing to health arrangements. But even more important than the practical issues are the emotional challenges. Change that is sudden and unanticipated is much harder to deal with, on an emotional level, than more gradual and incremental change. An anticipated retirement allows many months, if not years, of mental rehearsal. The individual who knows something is coming talks about it with others, anticipates potential problems, thinks about it, begins to notice others in the same situation, and gets mentally prepared for the new role in many subtle ways, well in advance of the actual transition. When the change is sudden, none of this mental preparation can occur.

All of this is especially difficult because one is dealing with two very different issues simultaneously: the health issues of a partner or spouse and the many complexities of terminating a career. In some cases the woman may actually be involved in terminating two careers, hers and his, while caring for a sick or dying spouse. These issues certainly arose for Katharine Hepburn as she gave up her career to care for Spencer Tracy. She was dealing, all at once, with the loss of his career, the loss of her career, and the tremendous burden of caring for someone who is sick and whose health is in continuous decline. It is hard to imagine a larger collection of serious issues to cope with simultaneously.

You May Have to Give Up Your Career Prematurely

When Katharine Hepburn stopped work to take care of Spencer Tracy, she was at the height of her career. She had just won an Academy Award nomination for *Long Day's Journey*

Into Night and was a major box office attraction. Indeed she was retiring at just the moment when no actor would choose to retire—her career was flourishing. Like so many women, her decision to retire was directed by the needs of her partner, not the natural flow of her career.

The Katharine Hepburn situation applies to many who stop working to take care of a family member or someone close to them. Not only has the career terminated unexpectedly, but that career may be still developing. Once again, this situation may occur more frequently for women than for men. A combination of factors makes it more likely that a woman might have to stop work at an earlier point in her career than a man might have to. First, for a couple, the average life expectancy of the man is shorter than that of a woman, so the health of the man may deteriorate at an earlier age. Second, for most couples the man is older than the woman to begin with. Finally, the woman's career may also have started later in her life than a man's. In many women's lives there is a long period of child raising responsibility and then more education before entering a career. According to Hudson, many women devote their young adult lives to raising a family and only later turn to a focus on career.[74] The woman may not only be giving up a career or job but may be leaving work having had a shorter time to engage in a working life, at a time when the career is still growing.

Work and Professional Connections May Be Lost

The person who stops work to care for an ill spouse may have to abandon virtually all work and professional connections. Precisely at the time when it might be valuable to maintain old ties, and to keep some continuity in the face of enormous upheaval, the demands of the situation may make that impossible.

This loss of professional connections may also mean a loss of resources for both emotional support and problem solving. The loss can be especially taxing if those professional connections were a major source of social support, as they are for many women.

Caring for the Seriously Ill Is Demanding

The fact that the retirement is involuntary, unplanned, unanticipated, and likely to be sudden is difficult enough in itself. But beyond that, you are now faced with caregiving responsibilities that in themselves may be extremely difficult. The physical demands of caregiving are often great. They are even more magnified by the fact that the person being cared for may have strong emotional needs as well as physical needs. And even beyond that, the demands of caregiving may lead to a spiraling isolation that removes many of the resources that could help one cope with this situation.

Anyone who has experienced a serious health problem knows that health concerns can overwhelm everything else. When our health is good, we take it for granted. When it is bad it totally dominates our lives.

For the person who is seriously ill, external demands are magnified at the same time internal resources are greatly diminished. Finances are strained, social networks dwindle, and a whole host of practical details need to be dealt with. At the same time, emotions may swing widely, problem solving abilities are crucial but impaired, energy and enthusiasm flag,

123

and the ability to cope with mundane activities may seem overwhelming.

This creates an extremely difficult situation for any caregiver. Caring for a gravely ill spouse is a profound physical and emotional burden. Virginia Richardson describes research that supports this conclusion:

> Recent research has now documented that care giving is inordinately stressful and takes a significant toll on women's lives. Emotional strains . . . include depression, anger, anxiety, frustration, guilt, sleeplessness, demoralization, feelings of helplessness, irritability, lower morale and emotional exhaustion. Other problems include disruptions in other relationships, inability to get out of the house, constant sleep interruptions. Caregiving . . . has deleterious effects on physical and mental health.[75]

Loss of Income and Financial Well Being

All of these changes can have a tremendous impact on finances. The illness of the spouse may mean the loss of the spouse's income, and on top of that the woman herself has found it necessary to give up her employment. Both of these losses may be unanticipated and unplanned for. On top of that the illness itself will impose major new expenses. If there are major financial burdens, this in turn can create further stresses. An unplanned reduction in financial status is one of the things people fear the most.

Grief and Reconstruction

If health problems lead to the death of the spouse, this produces a whole new set of serious difficulties. This is far more likely to happen to a woman than a man. The average life expectancy of a woman today is significantly longer than that of a man. For most couples the woman will outlive the man.[76] When this happens the woman has lost the person who may be her most significant life partner. The grief, sadness, loss, anguish, and emotional pain associated with the bereavement has the power to be crippling. The emotional toll can be devastating. One's life partner is gone. Constructing a new identity as a single person may be quite threatening. The grieving process is unique and different for all, but it is a process that may take months and years to work through. Some would say one never gets over it. But in any case, the loss is enormous. Additionally there may be two kinds of grief being experienced at the same time—the loss of a career and the loss of a spouse.

Beyond the profound emotional impact of the loss of a spouse, a whole host of other changes come into play. The woman has lost the partner she planned her future with. The social circles she once enjoyed with her spouse may now be awkward or impossible. She may have to construct a whole new identity, not an easy task at an advanced age. She is no longer part of a couple—she is a widow.

Coping with These Problems

We have argued that there is much in the lives of women that often makes their retirement more difficult than that of men. But in some ways women also seem to have an advantage over men. With women likely to face special difficulties, it is encouraging that there is much in the lives of women that prepares them to face these difficulties well.

Betty Friedan, writing in *The Fountain of Age*, was optimistic about women's abilities to cope with change. She pointed out that many women experience numerous "discontinuities" in their lives. To Betty Friedan, each of these discontinuities represents a kind of "retirement" that prepares women well for additional life changes to come.

> Some wives may retire as many as three different times during a lifetime. . . . From education to marriage, there is a strong role discontinuity; for the woman who disbands her work role to give priority to roles of mother and housewife; there is discontinuity when the children leave.[77]

Friedan believed that because of these numerous life changes, women have an advantage over men when it comes to adjusting to serious life transitions, including retirement. As evidence for this, Friedan cited a study showing that women between the ages of 50 and 60 who had returned to work or started work after raising children, had higher life satisfaction indices in later age. Their life satisfaction was higher than women who had a single continuous role — either homemaker or worker — throughout their adult life.[78] In summary Friedan argued that many women "have already had a lot of practice in involuntary retirement."[79]   She suggested that "the very discontinuity and change that has taken place in women's roles over a lifetime — their continual practice in retirement and disengagement, shift and reengagement"[80] might give them greater flexibility in resilience and prepare them for the many stressful changes they may face in aging.

This same resilience may help women deal with widowhood. Although the loss of a spouse is a traumatic experience, Friedan cited research showing that after a time:

> . . . the overwhelming majority became 'more independent and competent now than while their husbands were living' (63 percent); in addition, many became 'freer and more active' (47 percent) and 'more socially engaged' (31 percent). Only 18 percent viewed the major change in negative terms.[81]

This research suggests that many women seem to flourish after the death of their husband. They often "consider themselves fuller and freer people than before the death of their husbands." Friedan said this is not the case with men, who fare less well following the loss of a spouse.[82]

Nontraditional Relationships and Their Difficulty

Katharine Hepburn's relationship with Spencer Tracy was certainly not a traditional one. They were intimately involved with each other for more than a quarter century. They were clearly the most important person in each other's lives. Yet they were never married to each other. Spencer Tracy claimed that he never divorced his estranged wife Louise because of his Catholic religious beliefs, but he was such a complex character that it is almost impossible to know the real reason. Strangely, Hollywood's quintessential team of husband and wife on the screen were also a life-long couple off the screen—but not legally.

Many would find Tracy and Hepburn's relationship completely unacceptable. The legal description of their relationship would be that it is adultery and grounds for divorce. Most religious perspectives would define their relationship

127

as living in sin. Moreover, no matter how positively they described their relationship, it was a back street relationship that they felt compelled to hide. For 27 years they were afraid to publicly acknowledge their relationship. They knew their relationship had strong unacceptable dimensions to it. Few people back then, and few now, would approve of a married man with children living with someone else. Whatever one's view of their relationship, it was clearly an unconventional one and it illustrates some of the special problems that arise in nontraditional relationships.

Tracy and Hepburn's nontraditional relationship may have worked for them, but it was not without its costs. At the times of his illness and hospital stays, Kate faced awkward moments during visiting hours because she had no formally recognized role as a member of "the family." Hepburn's confusion about how to act at the time of Tracy's death is more evidence of the social awkwardness of her situation. She even found it so uncomfortable that she chose not to attend the funeral of her life-long partner. It seemed truly sad that the person who had cared so deeply and so well for Spencer Tracy all through his career and decline, had no "legitimate" right to assume a central role at the time of his death. It is evidence of the awkwardness that can be a component of relationships that exist outside the bounds of the traditional image.

The problems faced by nontraditional couples take on increasing prominence in our society as more and more people are electing to live in nontraditional relationships. Today more than half of all couples live together before marriage, and increasing numbers are choosing never to marry. But nontraditional relationships are not confined to the young—more and more older couples as well are choosing to live together without marriage. They do this for many reasons. For some, marriage late in life would produce financial disincentives, such as loss of certain pension benefits or loss of alimony. For others, they may have been married before and see no reason to marry again. Large numbers of gay and lesbian couples are unable to marry. Whatever the reason, living together in a nontraditional relationship produces special factors that need to be considered.

There are clearly practical and financial issues that nontraditional partners must pay special attention to. These include retirement accounts, life insurance, health insurance benefits, property taxes, income taxes, and inheritance of property. When one partner dies these issues take on a special prominence. It is very important to carefully plan what will happen with retirement funds and inheritance. These issues are very complex and vary from state to state according to financial laws. People in nontraditional relationships owe it to themselves to find out the laws and regulations that apply to their particular circumstance. Individual provisions need to be made to meet the legal requirements of each state, and these should be made in writing with appropriate legal counsel.

Spencer Tracy and Katharine Hepburn were wealthy, so the financial issues that often challenge a nontraditional relationship were never a concern for them. But even with all their money, they were still not free from the social discomforts that can accompany such a relationship. Although nontraditional relationships are increasingly common in our society, there are still many who respond very differently to a couple in a nontraditional relationship than to a married couple. While both partners are alive, they can confront these problems as a couple. But after the death of one partner, the lack of formal validation for the relationship can cause real problems. Will the non-married partner have difficulty staying in the house unless provisions have been made for this? Will there be tension between the surviving partner and members of the deceased partner's family with respect to family photographs, mementos, valued possessions, heirlooms, and family papers? Feelings can run extremely high regardless of the actual worth of the item: it may not matter whether it was a painting picked up on a trip to Italy or Grandfather's bamboo fishing rod; the emotional attachment of objects and mementos may overshadow their practical value.

A significant portion of retirement may be spent with one of the partners outliving the other. Retirement planning needs to take into account what will be done when there is only one person left. And this is especially complex when the relationship is a nontraditional one and the partners are not married. The issues involved should be anticipated and discussed in advance. Where possible they should be discussed with family and relatives, and where necessary they should be explicitly stated and put in writing.

Returning to Work

After giving up her career to take care of Spencer Tracy, Katharine Hepburn later found herself returning to work. For her this occurred in an unusual and spectacular fashion. She chose to make a final film with Tracy at the end of his life, and that film reignited her career. It allowed her to plunge back into acting with great energy following his death, leading to an enormously successful period, including three additional Academy Awards.

For most people, nothing so dramatic is likely to occur. However, it is surprising what large numbers of people will find themselves returning to some form of work following their initial "retirement." Statistics show more than half of all those who retire return to some kind of work within two years. For a variety of reasons many people miss the engaging challenge that accompanies a work life. For some it may be a return to part time work, for others it may be elevating a hobby to the level of a quasi-job, and for still others it is a chance to explore a kind of work or a volunteer commitment not possible when the bills had to be paid.

It is probably a mistake to conceptualize retirement as always a final and full turning away from all work and responsibility. Many people feel the need to use their creative and productive energy in ways that look and feel very much like a kind of "work." For many people, recreation and leisure are not meaningful enough alone. For them, some kind of meaningful productive work activity is desirable after retirement.

In planning for retirement, one need not think of a sudden and complete cessation of all work. Recognize that you may be one of the many people who discover, after a period of leisure, that leisure alone is not enough. It is advisable to plan for this at the outset. You may wish to retain some links with your present employer if that is an option. You also may want to think through in advance whether there may be other part-time or full-time work available that you would enjoy pursuing.

5

Jimmy Carter:
Reinventing a Life

Forced to Retire Before You Are Ready

An unanticipated or forced retirement is painful, but it can present an opportunity to reinvent your life. There are many ways in which a work-life can be terminated. For some, the transition into retirement is planned and expected; for others it is abrupt and painful. Research indicates that "forced" retirements are much more difficult to cope with than normal planned transitions. Common sense supports this conclusion. Not only does a forced termination from work have severe financial consequences, but it has potentially strong personal implications as well.

133

Dory Hollander devotes an entire chapter to this issue in her book about work-life cycles:

> Fired! For any employee that word feels like a bullet aimed straight at the heart. It shatters our stability and plays havoc with our identities. It wounds our self-esteem and destroys our sense of being part of a friendly and predictable world. No matter what the circumstances, it hurts.[1]

Hollander goes on to describe the feelings that characterize the many people she interviewed who had been involuntarily terminated from the world of work:

> After being fired, you'll enter an emotional whirlpool. Financial, social, familial, and personal pressures will swirl around you and sweep you away from making sense of what's happened. [You find yourself] recounting each detail of the firing as if understanding could free you of the horror.[2]

She describes a long list of words people use when they have been fired. These terms are mostly negative, such as: "disbelieving, shocked, betrayed, depressed, empty, insecure, anxious, angry, withdrawn, upset, violent, fearful, and ashamed."[3] Being fired is a powerful negative experience that is hard for anyone to cope with. It is easy to get stuck focusing on the wrong thing. The important question is "what next?" but it is hard to move past thinking about the "why did this happen?"

The emotional turmoil of being fired makes it hard to look forward to the next stage of one's life in a constructive way.

Bob Buford, in his book, *Half Time: Changing Your Game Plan from Success to Significance*, talks about the need for planning, the importance of setting priorities, and the strategies for maintaining control of the "second half" of your life (after age 50).[4] These opportunities for planning are eliminated or distorted by an unexpected termination. Being fired often leads to a period of being "off balance," and some people are never able to recover completely from such a calamity. The abrupt and unexpected termination of one's career can be the most intense test of one's character. It can severely challenge the ability to reorganize one's life.

One person whose career was dramatically terminated was Jimmy Carter, 39th president of the United States. Carter suffered a humiliating defeat in his 1980 reelection bid, which brought a sudden and unanticipated end to his political career. What makes him remarkable is that after a period of withdrawal and reflection, he made a dramatic personal recovery and became what many identify as our most impressive role model for productive retirement. Carter's story can teach us a great deal. He is a wonderful example of a person who, after a devastating experience, was able to completely reinvent his life.

The Backstory

James Earl Carter Jr. was born in 1924 in Plains, Georgia. He grew up in the nearby community of Archery, in a South Georgia farmhouse that had no electricity or running water. His father was a farmer and businessman and his mother was a nurse. Educated in public schools, he attended Georgia Southwestern College and the Georgia Institute of Technology. Earning a Bachelor of Science degree from the United States Naval Academy in 1946, he went on to do graduate work in nuclear physics.

He began a career in the United States Navy, serving with both the Atlantic and Pacific fleets, and rising to the rank of lieutenant. Following the death of his father he reexamined the direction his life was taking, and resigned his naval commission to return home.

Back in Plains, he and his wife Rosalynn operated a successful farm supply company, and established themselves as respected members of the community. He entered politics at the local level, and diligently worked his way up the political hierarchy. He ran successfully for a variety of elected positions, culminating in his election as the governor of Georgia in 1971. At this point in his life, at age 52, Jimmy Carter was already an American success story. In 1976, Jimmy Carter went on, in a dramatic upset, to defeat Gerald Ford and become the 39th president of the United States.

Losing the Presidency

Four years later in his bid for re-election, Jimmy Carter lost to Ronald Reagan. Many factors contributed to his loss, including the flagging economy, a period of raging inflation, a perceived decline of traditional moral values, decline of U.S. power overseas, and his inability to secure the release of American hostages in Iran. Carter's 1980 defeat was a resounding rejection by the voters—he carried only six of the 50 states. It was the first time an elected president failed to get re-elected since Hoover's defeat by Roosevelt 40 years earlier.

Not only did Carter lose the election, he lost his position as leader of the Democratic Party as well. By making his concession speech one hour before the western polls closed, he infuriated many Democratic leaders. Several candidates in the western sector felt that by conceding before their polls closed Carter caused them to lose their elections. Democratic house leader Tip O'Neill typified their angry reaction with his comment about the Carter team: "You guys came in like a bunch of jerks, and I see you're going out the same way."[5] Carter had been seen as a president most distanced from the influence, money and direction of the party. He had his own agenda. He was perceived as the "party-less president," but now this image seemed to work against him. In his loss he appeared to be totally without backing. The Democratic Party was quick to separate itself from the Carter debacle. Few presidents have seemed so alone in their defeat.

The loss was unexpected. Even many journalists failed to predict Carter's defeat. Personally, the Carters were shocked. They saw themselves on a kind of moral crusade and their loss felt like a personal rejection by the entire country. This was made even more painful because they were defeated by a politician they felt was immoral. Further, Reagan had campaigned on a promise to dismantle most of the programs the Carters had fought for. The Carters felt that the nation had rejected their most basic values. The defeat was resounding, public, and painful.

Back Home in Georgia

If the election loss was not devastating enough, Carter soon found out that the managers of his blind trust had mismanaged his money so badly that he was one million dollars in debt. When he and Rosalynn returned to Plains, Georgia to contemplate what to do with the rest of their lives, they felt as if they had gone from a life of promise and ability to one of emptiness and impotency. Jimmy Carter was 56 years old.

It is hard for ordinary people to imagine the shock and disorganization of a personal failure of this magnitude. Most of the world knew of his failure. There seemed to be no hiding place from the pain of it, and no expedient rationales to smooth it over. They had no option but to go home. Home to very ordinary things.

In their first project at home, he and Rosalynn personally installed a new floor in the attic of their Plains home. Carter was back where he started—out of work, one million dollars in debt, and without influence. He had gone from the very top of the American pyramid to the very bottom. He had gone from being the leader of the free world, to nailing down an attic floor in his home in Plains. The entire fall from grace and power had taken place in three short months.

The duties of office and transition of power had left little time to prepare or plan for the next stage of his life. Like Johnson, Nixon, and Ford before him, it would not have been surprising if Carter had faded into the relative oblivion of tinkering with a presidential library and a life of reclusive recreation. He came close to doing that. "He almost became a recluse," said his son Chip, "He considered becoming a missionary."[6]

This characterization may seem extreme, but Carter himself described his situation very similarly in his 1998 book, *The Virtues of Aging*. The first chapter of this book, titled "Kicked Out, Broke, but Fighting Back," describes the depth of his shock and disorganization:

> I was just fifty-six years old when I was involuntarily retired from my position in the White House. What made losing the job even worse was that it was a highly publicized event, with maybe half the people in the world knowing about my embarrassing defeat![7]

Carter talked about his own disappointment and his wife's discomfort with the abrupt change in their lives: "Rosalynn was especially bitter and angry, unable to accept with equanimity the result of the 1980 election."[8]

The Carters were dealt a paralyzing amount of adversity. Their lives were turned completely upside down. Hollander, writing about how people deal with terminations and early forced retirements, says it is particularly stressful when the person terminated felt good at the job they did and also liked doing that job. That certainly applied to Carter's situation. It seems logical that anyone running for the office of President of the United States, would have convinced himself (or herself) that he was the best qualified, and would be excited about the prospects of another term of office.

Much of the impact depends on how you felt. . . If you felt at home, then getting the boot means you're orphaned. You loved where you were, and you can't believe you're not there anymore. You feel isolated and betrayed. It's like losing your first love. It signifies the end of a dream. You ask yourself why it had to end like this.[9]

The loss the Carters encountered shook them at their most basic level. The word Jimmy Carter used to describe how they felt at that point in his life was "despair."[10] He said that his return to Plains was not a pleasant experience. He described it as a time when it was not easy to forget the past, or to overcome his fear of the future.

Rosalynn, even more than Jimmy, felt profoundly rejected. She thought they had been on a mission of good work that would surely meet the approval, not only of the members of the country, but of God himself:

"I don't understand it. I just don't understand why God wanted us to lose the election," I would say. Jimmy was always more mature in his Christian attitude than I was. He would say, "Do you think people are robots that God controls from heaven?"—or "You really don't think God orders things like this, do you? It's hard for us to accept the fact that our priorities are not the same as God's. We attach too much importance to things like popularity, wealth, and political success."[11]

Rosalynn went on to say, "I did finally learn to live with the results of the 1980 election, but I would never pretend that it came easily."[12] Easily indeed! Rosalynn not only had mental difficulty accepting the transition but once in Plains she started to have mysterious physical reactions to the stress as well.

> I began to have aches and pains. . . . My back hurt and
> my legs were stiff. When I got up from a chair I could hardly
> straighten up, as though I had been molded to fit it. I began to run
> a constant low-grade temperature. The pains got progressively
> worse, spreading to my neck and shoulders and then all over. . . .
> I had to give up my exercising and I started taking aspirin to ease
> the pain. The local doctor could find nothing wrong with me. I
> went to another, with the same result.[13]

Things continued to get worse until she checked herself in to a university clinic in Atlanta. The "mysterious affliction" continued to plague her. Steroids were suggested and rejected. Instead, she began an exercise program and some anti-inflammatory drugs in an attempt to "wear out" the malady. It took a long time. She reported that her spirits suffered and so did the book she was writing. In time, and with hard work, Rosalynn would "wear out" the disease. She reported, "I wondered then, and still do now, whether all the pent-up emotions from our defeat and our new circumstances could possibly have been the culprit for my illness."[14]

Both Carters entered a period of reflection, work, and recreation, becoming re-acquainted with their land, farm, home, and friends in Plains. It was difficult for two such accomplished and focused individuals to be so unsure of "what we would do with our remaining years."[15]

It also may have been a mild blessing, in disguise, that their funds had been mismanaged to the point where they felt in danger of losing their home and land. Having been so severely rejected by the public world of politics, it would have seemed enticing for them to say: well at least we have our home and private lives—we will just truncate our lives and spend the rest of our time "playing" in the security of our

142

private world. In the case of the Carters, the trauma of losing their professional standing was enlarged by the prospect that even their home and land were threatened. There really was no safe retreat. The Carters were facing losses in all of the major aspects of their lives.

A stroke of financial luck came their way when an expanding agricultural firm bought the Carter Warehouse. That, combined with a book contract, provided enough money for the Carters to keep their home and land. Always people with a strong sense of place, the Carters now seemed secure enough to freely contemplate their possible redefinition. Whatever this renaissance was to be, family, friends, and Plains would figure centrally in the adventure.

The starting point of the reflection, according to Carter, was asking himself "what were the things I really enjoyed doing in the past?"[16] Rosalynn seemed, at first, to have a more difficult time with the reorganization. "I was thinking our active life was over," she said. The grief and stress seemed to take a physical toll: "I just ached all over."[17] For Rosalynn, working in the yard and simple pleasures like jogging, biking, enjoying the seasons, looking for blackberries and picking plums seemed to occupy her enough to have a physically soothing effect.

Jimmy and Rosalynn expanded their range of activities as time moved on. They both took up downhill skiing in their late '50s. "I was so scared," Rosalynn said, "so scared, but then I got up there and I did it, and then I loved it."[18] The Carters always were, and remain, very physical people. In addition to the things mentioned above they enjoyed fishing, hunting, travel, mountain climbing, tennis, and (for him) making furniture. Some of these, like the skiing, came late in life and others like the fishing and hunting had been with them for decades.

For many people life full of such recreational pursuits would be a full life. But the Carters both knew that for them a life of pure recreation, without any goals they felt made a social contribution, would be unsatisfactory to them.

For an extended period of time the Carters worked on their memoirs and tried to figure out what the future held for them. But most of the reflection of this period was retrospective, not prospective. Putting the past in order was indeed a valuable task, but what to do with the future was a more formidable question—almost threatening in its scope, when compared to their successes of the past.

The Carters always had a strong supportive extended family. There were several family events and deaths that reminded them how much they valued the closeness of family ties and at the same time how difficult it is to find time to be together in a fast-paced modern world. They resolved to make their family an even stronger priority in their lives. Yearly reunions were planned with greater care and for extended periods of time. It was a daunting logistical problem to get the entire group of roughly 20 members together each year. The trips ranged from touring Disney World to camping in Belize. But even though family and recreation were important to the Carters, they felt the need to do more. Both Carters possessed a strong social conscience and a desire to do something more significant with the concluding chapters of their lives.

Describing their late life career changes, Carter said, "It wasn't easy." But he added, "We had made it several times when we were younger; why not now?"[19] For both of them, part of the answer lay in developing new careers—as writers, teachers, and health and human rights activists. For both Carters, happiness rested on having a purpose in life larger than themselves, and maintaining quality relationships with others.[20]

The Carter Center

When the Carters looked at what other ex-presidents had done with their post-presidential years, they found most examples unattractive. George Washington retired to be the "gentleman farmer" basking in the sun of an easy life. The activities of recent presidents seemed even less appealing. As one biographer put it:

> Ronald Reagan had sold the cachet of his U. S. presidency to the Japanese for 2 million in speaking fees; Gerald Ford spent much of this time in Palm Springs working on his golf swing while collecting director's fees from corporate boards; and Richard Nixon was holed up in New Jersey with his Dictaphone in a endless quest to remake his image from dirty crook to international sage.[21]

In fairness, there were a few models of ex-presidents who did do constructive things. Jefferson founded the University of Virginia. William Howard Taft taught law at Yale University, served as chairman of Woodrow Wilson's War Labor Board, and ultimately attained his lifelong goal of becoming Chief Justice of the United States Supreme Court. Herbert Hoover, although not widely admired for his presidency, was active well into his eighties, writing dozens of books, working at Stanford University's Institution of War, Revolution and Peace, and heading up two commissions intent on reorganizing the federal government. But these examples were unusual. Most ex-presidents directed their energy toward earning money, regaining the office of president, or reclusive leisure.[22]

The key to the Carters' reinvention of themselves, and establishing a new direction for the second half of their adult lives, arose out of their creative use of the concept of the presidential library. Establishing a presidential library, a center for the papers, recorded speeches, and documents of the presidency, has become tradition for former American chief executives. In one of the most peculiar of laws, in effect until the end of the Carter presidency, all the correspondence, records, documents, and mementos of a presidency belong personally to the president. It had been so since the time of George Washington. In the early years this involved a few boxes of material. In more recent years the collection of presidential papers and materials has become massive. In order to preserve the history of our nation the law now provides that once presidents raise funds from private contributions for the construction of a library to house such documents and articles, the library is then deeded over to the federal government, which will maintain it in perpetuity.

In recent times presidents and their heirs have used this notion creatively. The Roosevelt and Kennedy libraries were innovative for their time. The Kennedy Library, beautifully designed by architect I. M. Pei, was picturesquely set by the water's edge near the University of Massachusetts campus. Both libraries extended the notion of a presidential "library." These libraries were places visitors could step back into the history of the period. They were museums as well as libraries. The Carters wanted to formulate a plan that would go even further, creating a presidential library that would be much more than just a library or even a museum.

What exactly to do with the library "concept" was not yet clear. Jimmy Carter was adamant that his presidential library was not to be a monument to him. He had turned down several architectural plans that inclined in that direction. Carter had some vague notion that his presidential library should be some sort of "teaching center." But the thought was ill-formed in his mind. Nevertheless he stubbornly refused to return to the concept of a traditional library. Then came the revelation. In *Everything to Gain,* Rosalyn describes waking one night to find her husband sitting up in bed, excited about new plan for the library:

> I know what we can do at the library. . . . We can develop a place to help people who want to resolve disputes. There is no place like that now. If two countries really want to work something out, they don't want to go to the United Nations and get one hundred fifty other countries involved in the argument . . . . We could get good mediators that both sides would trust, and they could meet with no publicity, no fanfare, perhaps at times in total secrecy. If there had been a place like that I would not have had to take Begin and Sadat to Camp David.[23]

Rosalynn and Jimmy found themselves energized as they continued to develop this new idea. It was good to have direction again. On a trip to Hawaii they rose well before dawn, because of the time change, and talked for hours about this new design. The Carter Center would be much more than simply a place to house papers for scholars or a museum of the times. The Carters began to flesh out an entirely new vision for their library. It would be a home for social action: a center for conflict resolution, a center for monitoring and promoting human rights issues, a center for education on worldwide health issues, and a center to promote democracy and democratic elections around the globe. Because of the way the law was written, if the Carters could raise the money to make the library operational, federal funds could be used to maintain it. In a sense Carter could once again become a partner with the American people in completing his unfinished agenda as president.

In 1983 the Carters launched their initial concept for the Carter Center, a think tank for ideas about peaceful resolution of conflicts worldwide. The Carter Library had been incorporated in 1981, but it took several years and a few false starts before the full vision of the center began to fall into place. The Carters wanted a center that would be an active meeting place where people would come to a quiet comfortable retreat in a beautiful setting, a place where one could engage in reflection, spirituality, and planning. But they also wanted it to be more than that. They wanted a place that would be a dynamic center for active conflict management, "a place where people could gather to discuss issues and ideas, pursue a common dream, or resolve long-standing differences in a beautiful and peaceful setting."[24] Rosalynn reflects on this transition period in *Everything to Gain*:

> We had to work our way through various stages—self-pity, anger, discouragement, anxiety. But after . . . [a] somewhat painful readjustment, we had come to accept our new circumstances. Finally we made the exciting discovery that our lives do not need to be limited to past experiences. The future could be challenging and fulfilling as well.[25]

Putting his programs under the umbrella of the Carter Center was a brilliant stroke in several ways. It allowed many of the programs to receive direct or indirect support from federal financing. Even more important, it institutionalized the programs in ways that would allow them to continue well beyond his own lifetime.

Carter had watched, with dismay and anger, as Reagan systematically dismantled a whole host of social and environmental programs that he had initiated. Some examples were: allowing sales of oil leases in environmentally sensitive areas, allowing grain sales to countries that violated human rights, supporting international loans to some countries with dictatorships or flagrant human rights abuses, embracing dictatorships, eliminating federal funds to help states and cities buy land for parks, reducing federal spending on Basic Education Opportunity Grants and student loans.[26]

Now Carter could establish programs that would not be subject to the whims of a future administration. Another advantage was that he could now advocate for his causes without always having to worry about competing considerations. Unlike when he was president, he would not have to balance a human rights issue with whether a country was a major oil supplier to the West, or balance environmental causes with the demands of industry. In some ways he would be freer than he ever was as president to have a major impact on human affairs.

The Carter Center remains one of the most creative things to come out of the Carter presidency. It had the potential to eclipse the accomplishments of his somewhat dismantled four-year presidential term. As Douglas Brinkley pointed out in his book, *The Unfinished Presidency*, this was the beginning of Carter's pilgrimage to complete his unfulfilled hopes for his presidency. "Jimmy Carter may be many things, but a quitter is not among them — so . . . his presidency will remain unfinished as long as he is alive."[27] This was the mission the Carters needed to refocus their energy and time. And it would be fully under their control, free of all the posturing and political considerations that go with elected office.

It may not have been clear to the Carters at first, but the conceptualization of the Carter Center revived the hopes and plans that had motivated them their entire lives. This was possible because they had such a powerful drive to do something that mattered. This was not to be a retirement to a rocking chair, or to reclusive recreation, but to a renewed dedication to finish the work of their lives. From the relatively free perspective of retirement, they could do what they felt mattered without the constraints and posturing of political life.

In the years since Jimmy Carter was turned out of office, his private and professional contributions have grown exponentially. His list of accomplishments in "retirement" seems more impressive than those completed before his forced retirement. Arguably only Jefferson, Taft and Hoover come close to Carter in post-career achievements. It would take an entire book to chronicle this impressive adventure. A few highlights follow.

Since losing the presidency Jimmy Carter has published 24 books; including two revisions of earlier books. The list of published books includes: *Keeping Faith: Memoirs of a President*, 1982, 1995; *Negotiation: The Alternative to Hostility*, 1984; *The Blood of Abraham*, 1985, 1993; *Everything to Gain: Making the Most of the Rest of Your life* (with Rosalynn), 1987, 1995; *An Outdoor Journal*, 1988, 1994; *Turning Point: A Candidate, a State, and a Nation Come of Age*, 1992; *Talking Peace: A Vision for the Next Generation*, 1993, 1995; *Always a Reckoning*, (poetry) 1994; *The Little Baby Snoogle-Fleejer* (children's book, with Amy Carter) 1995; *Living Faith*, 1996; *Why Not the Best*, 1975 (revised in 1996); *A Government as Good as its People*, 1977 (revised in 1996); *Sources of Strength: Meditations of Scripture for a Living Faith*, 1997; *The Virtues of Aging*, 1998; *Atlanta: The Right Kind of Courage*, 2000; *An Hour Before Daylight: Memoirs of a Rural Boyhood*, 2001; *Christmas in Plains*, 2001; *The Personal Beliefs of Jimmy Carter*, 2002 (compilation of previous works); *The Hornet's Nest*, 2003; *Sharing Good Times*, 2004; *Our Endangered Values*, 2005; and *Palestine: Peace Not Apartheid*, 2006.

These books are vast in range. They cover politics, poetry, political philosophy, negotiation and peaceful conflict management, advice on life, advice on aging, a children's book, a sportsman's journal, and history. Many of the books were on best seller lists for long periods of time. Recently, he became the first president to write a novel and the first president to write a sex scene in a novel (even if it was only one sentence). He even painted the art for the cover!

This list of books published since losing the presidency is an extraordinary set of accomplishments. Few published authors could boast such a list over a lifetime. It is even more impressive that these books were all written since his retirement. Standing alone, this would serve as a monumental achievement, but when placed against the numerous other accomplishments of Jimmy Carter, it becomes astounding.

While doing all this writing, Carter was extremely active with a whole variety of other activities. These included: establishing the Carter Center for Conflict Resolution; creating the Carter Presidential Library; teaching as University Distinguished Professor at Emory University; establishing the Global 2000 program to advance health and agriculture in the developing world; launching The Atlanta Project to attack social problems associated with poverty; creating his own, world wide, campaign to eliminate hunger; starting a separate world wide campaign to eliminate poor nutrition and guinea worm; monitoring elections in numerous third world nations; establishing the Freely-Elected Heads of Government (an organization to monitor free and fair democratic national elections); serving as an international arms control consultant; traveling around the world as a consultant and speaker; serving as a church deacon and Sunday School teacher; and supporting the work of Habitat for Humanity. In his personal life he painted, fished, wrote poetry and worked at carpentry for fun and charity.

The culminating accolade for Carter, and perhaps the highest international recognition anyone could receive, came on December 10, 2002. Jimmy Carter was awarded the Nobel Peace Prize. In awarding the prize, the chairman of the Norwegian Nobel Committee said Jimmy Carter was "one of the most deserving and least controversial Laureates for a long time. . . . [He] has contributed in practically all the areas that have figured most prominently through the one hundred and one years of Peace Prize history."[28]

Looking at this enormous list of accomplishments, one feels almost overwhelmed. Carter is more than an ordinary role model. He is more like an apotheosis of all that this stage of life could be. Indeed one wonders if, when all the history is in, Carter's post presidency years may actually be more significant and enduring than his Presidency itself.

Carter himself seems aware of all this. When asked if he would still like to be president in a 1997 CSPAN interview with Kathleen Quindlan, Carter responded: "If I were offered the presidency now and didn't even have to run for it, I still would rather head up the Carter Center." Additionally Carter seems to have truly found a deeper sense of personal satisfaction:

> This is the happiest time of my life. . . . I have no burning ambitions. I don't have anything to fear now. . . . I never really liked the political world, the posturing, the appealing for votes, the tailoring of answers. . . . I feel truer to myself. I'm more a missionary than a politician. I am where I really belong.[29]

LIFE AFTER WORK

What the Jimmy Carter Story Tells Us

The Carter story has much to tell us about guidelines for effective retirement. It should be noted first that Carter's situation was unique. It had many components that most of us will never experience, and that may never again come together in the particular way they did for Jimmy Carter. Having the resources of a former president of the United States at your fingertips, an ability to generate considerable sums of money, and the enormous support system the Carters enjoyed, are rare indeed. Their story is not a "model" that can be applied to a general population. Still, what it can tell us about retirement is instructive. There are basic lessons here that can speak to the problems we all face in this life transition. The Carter saga exemplifies a set of principles that can instruct and inform many people entering the second half of life—even if they enter that stage unprepared, unplanned, and off balance.

Unexpected Retirement Is Often Painful and Difficult

The Carter story tells us that even for people with enormous talent and resources an unanticipated retirement is painful and difficult. It took the Carters several years to create a plan for what they wanted to do in their retirement. Their first reactions were shock, dismay, loss, bitterness, and anger. There were even serious health problems that may have been caused in part by this traumatic change. In the Carters' own words:

Retirement can be one of life's greatest dangers if all we do is brace ourselves to face what we think will be many barren and useless years. At worst, there are some who lose the will to live, especially those who have been very ambitious or productive in earlier years. They fear a monotonous life without purpose—and without respect from others.[30]

It is hard to imagine a couple being dealt a more crippling blow than the Carters. But the situation can be hopeful. Seeing their recovery is inspiring and informative.

Unexpected Retirement Provides Opportunities

The Carters are living proof that retirement, planned or unplanned, presents an exciting set of opportunities for redefinition. Once a person can get past the pain and loss of the "old life," the new opportunities are indeed exciting and invigorating. We are sure that even Carter himself would not have predicted in 1981, that he would say in 1998, that he was now in the "happiest time of his life." When asked if he would like to be President again, Carter's response was that he found his post-presidential life to be much more rewarding, productive, satisfying, and in keeping with his true nature. He went so far as to say that he would not want to be President again even if it were given to him. This is a bright shinning example of actualized potential. While the Carters may not be a model, they most surely are a beacon.

Give Yourself Time

It seems important to provide a period of reflection, review and redefinition after a major life trauma such as the unexpected termination of a career. Like all good problem solvers, the Carters provided themselves with time: time to grieve their loss, time to respect their own feelings, time to assess their strengths and weaknesses, and time to clear away the obstacles to a positive transition. It was important, for the Carters, to take the necessary time and not rush into another venture simply for lack of a role. In fact, the act of writing their memoirs and autobiographies provided Rosalynn and Jimmy Carter an excellent reflective tool to clearly understand where they had been and what they liked, and did not like, about the part of their lives they had just finished. The Carters were not ready to plan the second half of their life when the first half ended. They needed some time. Even though we might like it to happen quickly, the transition to a new life stage should not be rushed.

Know What Is Important to You

Perhaps the most valuable guideline we can get from the Carters' experience is the need to know what things are important to you personally. This is different for every person. For the Carters, it became clear to them that living a full and rich life meant more than recreation. Similarly, although family was very important to them, a life devoted to family would not have been enough. It was critical for the Carters to continue to make a broader contribution. The Carters also knew that, for them, their life plans would seem incomplete unless they took into account their strong concern with justice and social issues.

The Carters were relentless in their search for a personal understanding about what was important to them. Indeed, the entire book *Everything to Gain* was a rumination on this theme, and the process of writing it was hard for them. Jimmy said in an interview that this book, jointly written by him and his wife, almost broke up their marriage. The task was so difficult and contentious at points that their editor had to rescue them with a plan to put the initials "J" and "R" before paragraphs that contained opinions they didn't share. But in the Carters' case, the payoff for struggling through this was enormous. They were able to discover what they enjoyed doing, what they wanted to accomplish with the rest of their lives, what resources they had, and what new resources they needed. In our opinion this exercise was the linchpin of their transition to successful retirement.

The Carter story makes clear that it is extremely important to know and understand yourself. Many professions force a person into a required mold instead of drawing on and extending the natural skills, gifts, and personal leanings we all have. In his book *Half Time*, Bob Buford presents that notion that the "second half" of our lives is when we should move from concern with *success* to concern with *significance*. The retirement phase of life offers us one more chance to "get it right." Our satisfaction in our remaining years will depend on doing the things that are most significant and meaningful to us. What these are may vary greatly from person to person. For all of us, however, discovering significance is important and requires thought and examination.

For the Carters, writing their individual autobiographies was a wonderful way to engage in the reflection and re-examination process. Few would have conducted such an extensive life review process. There are other ways we could use to discover what is important to us: conversations with friends or spouse, contemplation of the things we are most proud of, reflection on what brings the greatest satisfaction. We could engage in a systematic planning process, or we could go through a less systematic period of trying new things. What the Carter story shows is how important it is to conduct *some* review process, to think carefully about the things that are most meaningful to us personally, and to plan a retirement that makes those things central.

Planning Can Be Important

The unanticipated onset of their retirement must have been particularly hard for the Carters, who had carefully planned almost every aspect of their lives. It is significant that it took the Carters several years to clarify opportunities and construct new goals. Even though the Carters had little opportunity to make arrangements in advance, they eventually constructed a comprehensive plan.

Once back in Plains, Georgia, after their unexpected exodus from the White House, they devoted long hours to careful discussion of what they wanted to do with their lives. Aware that they wanted this next period of their lives to be meaningful and constructive, they did not allow themselves to just drift into what was most convenient or most pleasant. The Carters wanted to develop a new and different agenda. To do that effectively they needed to do some creative planning. This would take time and lots of effort. In many ways it resembled the starting of a career more than the ending of one. In fact it was a new beginning.

The Carters believed, and we agree, that it is dangerous to assume a good retirement will just "happen on its own." You need to be in charge of it. The Carters' thoughtful, systematic examination of how they wanted to spend their retirement years provides a strong example for those who want to do something productive and creative with their retirement years.

Attending to the Three R's

Carter is also a good example of a person who seemed to have a good sense of attending to what we call the "Three R's of Retirement." This concept is more fully explained at the end of Chapter Three. The "Three R's" are: Relationships, Responsibilities, and Recreation. Carter's life has a healthy balance of close attention to each of these areas.

He works hard at his *Relationships* with his wife, children, friends, and colleagues. He exhibits a fundamental awareness that one's network of relationships requires attention and forms the most fundamental basis for one's sense of personal happiness. In his books he often discusses the importance of family and friends. He has even co-authored books with his wife, and daughter Amy. Planning the yearly family retreats and adventures are important to him. The Carter family is a rich and diverse network of people who support each other and bring a constant sense of enrichment into each other's lives. As in all the areas of his life, Carter gives his relationships careful reflection and attention.

160

The *Responsibilities* part of this triangle is most clearly and overtly demonstrated in Carter's post-presidential life. He works with his church, Habitat for Humanity, The Carter Center for Conflict Resolution, and on world campaigns to eliminate hunger and disease, to promote health, and to support fair elections in developing countries. The list could go on and on. Carter in his "retirement" is ten times more productive than most people at the apex of their professional lives. He is widely admired for his energetic commitment to so many important causes. Carter is consistently ranked highest as the retiree that is most respected by other retired people. His credit here is well deserved.

Recreation is the area that comes to mind most quickly when most people think of retirement. For many, retirement is only about recreation. Carter has always had a healthy attitude toward his recreational life. Even while President he found time to fish, hunt and work in the White House carpentry shop. It is hard to believe that someone with so many accomplishments in other significant areas of his life is also so richly developed in this area. He found time to write a book of poetry, paint, fish, hunt, make furniture, publish two editions of an outdoor journal, and even learned to ski after the age of 50.

We feel it is a credit to Carter that he has managed to accomplish so much, attend to the important people in his life, and enjoy a rich collection of recreational activities. His life looks purposeful, caring, and fun—all at the same time. He is a great example of someone who has brought the "Three R's" into balance.

Character Counts

One important factor that contributed to Jimmy Carter's successful retirement was the quality of his character. Perhaps the most striking characteristic that served Carter well was his extraordinary self-discipline, focus, and tenacity. Peter Bourne is a psychiatrist who was Jimmy Carter's top advisor on health and drug abuse for 18 months and has written a comprehensive biography of his former boss. When asked what Carter's greatest strengths and weaknesses were, he responded,

> I think his greatest strength is absolutely extraordinary tenacity. Where other people saw only obstacles and insurmountable hurdles, Carter would set his eyes on a goal and it was as though he had an inner compass, and he would drive for that goal relentlessly and nothing would make him give up.[31]

Carter also seems to be blessed with an unusually high energy level. Put simply, Carter seems to have more energy than most of us. When his willingness to work 16 hour days is combined with his drive, his tenacity, his careful cultivation of good habits, his commitment to excellence, and his clear sense of direction, an enormous amount can be accomplished.

A final character trait that had a major impact on the direction of Carter's retirement was his concern with justice and social issues. He gives this advice on planning for retirement: "Search for what is unseen—happiness, justice, friendship, intimacy."[32] He seems most energized when his faculties are fully engaged in meeting some worthy challenge head-on. For Carter it was important to employ the full use of his power along lines of social justice and personal dignity.

His friend Andrew Young described Carter as one of those rare men who live their lives knowing they have only a limited time to make a lasting contribution. "We all know that our lives are going to end," said Young, "but we don't live that way. Great men are the ones who do. Franklin Roosevelt, Martin Luther King, and Jimmy Carter all [were such men]."[33]

Carter's example of self-discipline, focus, and energy can serve as an inspiring example for all of us. Certainly having such a positive role model for these characteristics as Jimmy Carter might serve to inspire others to engage the "better angels of our nature" in service of this difficult transition.

Spirituality and Life Purpose

In attempting to understand the Carter story, it is important to recognize the Carters' sense of spirituality and life purpose. A close Carter associate told us that it is impossible to understand the Carters unless one understands their central life motivation, which derives from their strong grounding in Southern Baptist evangelical training. This training is connected to a sense of good works, a commitment to helping others, a sense of dedication to those less fortunate, and a passion for community and social justice. This is a consistent theme throughout Jimmy Carter's life and was a driving force in his political life. Oddly, he is much freer to pursue these goals from the Carter Center than he was from the office of the Presidency, with all its political constraints and deal-making.

The Carters' sense of purpose is driven by their religious convictions. Even in their time of deepest confusion they knew that whatever they did in retirement would be oriented around their sense of concern for others and their desire to leave the world a better place. A successful retirement (and life) for them would have to be one in which they made a significant contribution to cultural, social, and humanitarian ends. They seem to have succeeded amazingly well.

The Carter story tells us that some fundamental, ethical or spiritual grounding is helpful in guiding us through the second half of adult life. For some it may be religion, for others it may be a sense of family and tradition, for others it may be a set of personally meaningful values. No matter what the source, some orientation larger than personal comfort or self absorption provides a sense of direction and a greater satisfaction in this period of life transition and development.

Optimism and Sense of Control

In one of the most comprehensive reviews of scientific findings on factors that lead to personal happiness, David Myers said that a major factor leading to life satisfaction is having an optimistic attitude and a sense of personal control over one's life.[34] The Carter story suggests that optimism and a sense of control were critical to their successful retirement transition.

Even in the most difficult periods of their transition to a successful retirement, Carter retained an overarching sense of optimism, a sense of control over his life, and perhaps because of that, a willingness to take risks. Carter seems well aware of this issue.

> I have always enjoyed difficult challenges. At the same time I have faced the realization that it is not easy to take a chance or confront the prospect of failure and embarrassment. But my feeling is that if we refuse to try something that might fail, we lack faith either in ourselves or in our causes and goals.[35]

164

In an interview in Business Week in 1998, he said that "For us, retirement has not been the end but a new beginning. We hope to spend many more years actively making the most of the rest of our lives."[36] In the conclusion to their book *Everything to Gain*, the Carters emphasize how important it is

> . . . not to be afraid of advancing age. This late period can be a time of foreboding and resignation. . . . But it also offers the chance to be bolder than ever before and to do worthwhile things that have been avoided or postponed for five or six decades. To take that chance is what this book is really meant to encourage.[37]

The Carters offer us this advice: "We need a sense of control over our lives if we are to avoid being resigned to defeat or failure." He says, " We need to be confident that a full and enjoyable life with its share of successes is possible if we are willing to meet the challenges head-on."[38]

6

Arthur Ashe:
Coping with Adversity

When Your Health Fails You

One thing everyone thinks about when they start to consider retirement is their health. Often our images and expectations about this important issue are quite unrealistic. Some people assume—and fear—that they are soon to be candidates for a nursing home. Others, especially those who have worked hard on their general health and well being, seem to deny the possibility that their years in later life will have any health problems at all.

For most people the true picture lies somewhere between these two extremes. The research shows that a relatively small portion of the population will spend any extended period of time in a nursing home. Contrary to the fearful image, often fueled by unflattering portrayals of the elderly in films and the news media, most senior citizens lead active lives filled with rich possibilities. The image of the elderly as debilitated and needing extended care in a nursing home is not an accurate one. The vast majority of the elderly spend the largest portion of later age independent, fully able to care for themselves and enjoy a satisfying life.

The second perception, that later age will be one of problem-free health, may be just as unrealistic. Some lucky few will enjoy an advanced age with no health problems, but the aging process does exact a toll. The old canard is probably true: "anyone who says he can do everything at 60 he could do at 30 probably wasn't doing much at thirty." With aging, for most of us, comes some loss of energy and vitality. Things slow down. There are more aches and pains. For many, health issues that were minor at a younger age start to become more significant. Your body at 70 simply isn't what it was at twenty.

Even so, most seniors are able to enjoy full lives if they so choose. As Betty Friedan asserted in her book *The Fountain of Age,* the big difference between those who thrive in later age and those who do not is often the *attitude* they bring to the experience. While relatively minor health setbacks propel some people into a preoccupation with matters of health and inactivity, others are able to live rich full lives to the end, even while facing serious maladies and health problems that come along with the aging process.

Up to this point in our book we have not considered this important issue. All of the principle figures profiled in this book so far enjoyed good health, some — like the Delany sisters — to an extraordinary degree. It may be overly optimistic to hope for that. Few of us will reach eighty, ninety or one hundred in such good condition. For many ordinary people, coping with health problems in advanced age will be a necessity. The challenge that many of us will face is not having that adversity overwhelm the constructive possibilities of retirement and aging. What we are about to explore is a story and a life of extraordinary courage and grace in the face of just such a challenge.

One group of people for whom health is particularly important is athletes. Their career depends on their body. They know that a minor injury for an ordinary person could, in their case, end their career. If they are lucky, they will stay healthy throughout their career and not have an injury that cuts it short. But athletes know that even in the best of circumstances, there will come a time when their body will begin to let them down, and their career as an athlete will have to come to an end. For them it is always a race against the clock. Even for the greatest of athletes, their moment in the sun will be relatively brief. They will be faced with the prospect of finishing their athletic career well before they reach the normal "retirement" age.

If we think of retirement as a transition to the "second half" of adult life, this transition will occur earlier for athletes than for most of us. But the same factors will come into play. A person who has a career, and who may define himself or herself largely in terms of that career, now needs to make a transition to another phase of life. For many, this transition is not only a career transition, but a transition to another identity. For athletes this kind of transition comes early, and it may be extremely difficult.

The role of luck, or chance, or fate, plays a big part when it comes to our health. Some of us will face serious health problems. Very few of us know exactly what those will be or

169

when they will come. This raises the question of how we will respond when a turn of events occurs that we were not fully prepared for—and perhaps *could* not be fully prepared for. Do any of us really know what we would do if we found out tomorrow that we had a life-threatening illness? How does one react when bad news strikes?

People have very different reactions. Some may rage against their fate; others may live in denial; and still others miraculously rise to the challenge of coping with tremendous adversity and living their lives with optimism and a sense of control in the face of physical decline.

Those who knew Arthur Ashe regard him as a wonderful example of grace under pressure. His story is almost larger than life. A world-class tennis player, his tremendous success on the court was matched and even eclipsed by his contributions off the court. He was one of those rare people who lived his life to the fullest even as fate continued to deal him serious blows. His is a story of fame, courage, transition, and bad luck. It is also a story of elegance, kindness, and dignity that few have achieved.

The Backstory

Early Years

A statue honoring Arthur Ashe stands on Monument Avenue in Richmond, Virginia, the city where he grew up. Ashe is portrayed holding a tennis racket in one hand, and a book in the other. This statue depicts two of his lifelong attributes — his love of tennis and his love of ideas. Both of these sides of Arthur Ashe had their formative beginnings as he grew up poor and black in the segregated "Jim Crow" South.

Arthur Ashe was born on July 10, 1943, in Richmond, the city that was once the capital of the Confederacy. He grew up in a small home at the edge of a park, one of several set aside for African Americans in the segregated city. His father was a special policeman in charge of the park. He was only six when he started to play tennis on the courts behind his house, but his natural talent soon became evident.

Ashe's mother, Mattie, taught him to read before he entered school, creating a love of books and ideas that would later culminate in the authorship of many books. He later recalled, "many days as a kid I'd turn on soft music and read all day."[1] The intellectual sensitivities excited by his mother would be with him his entire life. Although he was a wonderful athlete, he would never be *only* an athlete. He would always value his intellectual side, and his commitment to social causes, even more than he valued his considerable athletic success.

Parents and Values

Arthur Ashe's life changed forever when he was not quite seven years old. His mother was hospitalized during her third pregnancy. It was a Saturday morning when his father came into the bedroom and woke Arthur and his younger brother Johnnie. Distraught and sobbing, he pulled both boys close to him and told them that during the night their mother had died.[2] It was an unexpected and wrenching turning point for their small family. From this point on, everything would be different.

Years later the memory of his mother was still very much with him as wrote the first pages of his autobiography, **Days of Grace:** "Every day since then I have thought about her. I would give anything to stand once again before her, to feel her arms about me, to touch and taste her skin. She is with me every day, watching me in everything I do."[3] Throughout his life, when a crucial decision had to be made that would require character and integrity, he would ask himself this question: what would his mother think if he didn't make the right decision?[4]

Arthur Ashe's father now served the role of both parents to his sons. Although that would be difficult for any parent, his father was up to the task. A strong believer in the value of hard work, he provided a role model of discipline and character. When not on duty as a special policeman, he was often at work at one of his many other jobs—catering, cooking, or taking care of gardens. He took pride in doing every job as well as he could. Arthur gradually began to adopt his father's values. As a young man, he helped his father construct a new home made almost entirely with material discarded from a nearby construction project.[5]

Ashe's father was a strict disciplinarian—his word was law, and he enforced the law with his thick police belt.[6] Arthur and his brother were not allowed to spend their time frivolously. Their father measured how long it should take them to get home from school, which was exactly 12 minutes, and if they were late they had better have a good explanation. One explanation that was acceptable was some service to others, such as helping an elder member of the community. Their father taught them that helping others was important, and modeled it as well. Along with his sons, he distributed old clothes, food, and wood to families that needed it.

Another lesson Ashe took from his father was the importance of getting along with others. His father believed in standing up for his rights but not being personally offensive in the process. He told Arthur and his younger brother Johnnie to avoid making enemies, and that "you gain by helping others."[7] Ashe was encouraged to be respectful of others and to value getting along. He was taught these values daily through the example and insistence of his father.

Ashe always had an intense concern about his reputation. His posthumously published autobiography, *Days of Grace,* begins with these words:

> If one's reputation is a possession, then of all my possessions, my reputation means most to me. Nothing comes even close to it in importance. Now and then, I have wondered whether my reputation matters too much to me; but I can no more easily renounce my concern with what other people think of me than I can will myself to stop breathing.[8]

For Ashe, this concern with how others saw him was intimately connected to the concept of service. Ashe's father instilled in him a commitment to making a difference in the world.

> I guess I was different from most other athletes, especially in tennis, because I knew that a lot of people expected much from me, and that if I disappointed them, it would be extremely painful to them, and to me.[9]

Natural Talent

Ashe's talent at the game of tennis was apparent when he was very young. Ron Charity, Richmond's best black tennis player, was practicing on the court behind Ashe's home and noticed six year old Arthur watching him. He sensed the boy's interest and invited him to hit a few balls. Inspired by Charity's interest, Ashe determined to learn the game of tennis. He began to work with Charity and continued to play under his supervision. One day while practicing, he was noticed by Dr. Robert Johnson, a tennis advocate, who coached promising black youths. Each summer Dr. Johnson invited some of these players to his camp in Lynchburg, and soon Arthur was spending summers there. His game continued to improve, and he began traveling more and more to compete first in local, then regional, and finally national tournaments. In 1955, he won the national 12-and-under black tennis championship. He began to enter tournaments for whites, although many—including those in his home town—would not accept entries from African Americans.

In 1960, he moved to St. Louis, Missouri, to live with a friend of Johnson's and play tennis year round. Soon he won a major tournament in which he was the only black player. Even with his busy tennis schedule, he continued to excel in his studies, and he graduated from high school with the highest grades in his class. His tennis skill, combined with his academic talent, led to a scholarship offer. The University of California at Los Angeles, a powerhouse of college tennis that produced many champions, offered Ashe the first scholarship it had ever given a black tennis player.

At UCLA his success as a rising tennis star was intermingled with reminders of his roots in poverty. He was doing well academically, traveling with a highly respected team, winning tournaments, and even playing with stars like Dinah Shore at the Beverly Hills Tennis Club, but at the same time he was facing difficulties that many of his classmates were not.

In his sophomore year at UCLA, Ashe didn't have enough money to return home to Virginia for the Christmas vacation. His tennis coach J.D. Morgan had invited Ashe to his home for Christmas. He was grateful for the invitation, but he refused, thinking he would be intruding on the Morgan family. The college dining service had shut down for the holiday. On Christmas Eve, he had barely enough money to get a sandwich out of a vending machine in the basement of the dorm, and he spent the evening alone in his room. The experience of spending this typically joyous holiday alone and broke made a strong impression on the young student athlete. He recalled this incident in his 1981 memoir, *Off the Court*:

> I wasn't tempted to run out and steal anything, but I thought long and hard about what it meant to have no money at all for an extended period. I was determined to never be in that situation again.[10]

Combining Tennis with Social Action

His tennis success continued. He was undefeated during his freshman year, and at the age of 20 he was named to the Davis Cup team to represent the U.S. around the world. At 21, he won the national collegiate tennis championship. Throughout this time, race continued to be an issue for Ashe. As a youth he had been denied access to segregated tennis courts, barred from white tennis clubs, and excluded from many tournaments on the basis of race. Because Ashe was so good, and virtually alone as a superlative black tennis player, the burden of confronting racial discrimination often fell on his shoulders. A clear example of this arose when he was at UCLA. The Balboa Bay Club of Orange County had invited the UCLA tennis team to play in its annual tournament, but would not allow Ashe to play because he was black. His coach told Ashe that if he wanted them to, the team would stand with him and refuse to play "We don't have to send the team," the coach said, "it is up to you."[11] Ashe had to make a choice. Was he prepared to follow through with total commitment to this issue? He remembered his father's advice that he must become an example of excellence so that one day tennis would be available to everyone. He made the decision not to protest the club's rules at that time. His decision was based on a complex set of considerations: in part it was concern over a career that was just beginning; in part it was concern for his fellow teammates; in part it was respect for a coach that he admired; in part it honored his father's advice not to needlessly make enemies on his way up. He didn't want to get drawn into making racial protest the center of his life at this point. He felt he first needed to devote his full energy to becoming the best tennis player he could possibly be.

Although he chose not to confront racism directly, he believed his success on the court was a contribution to the fight against racial injustice. He was determined not only to do well, but to conduct himself in a manner he felt would bring honor to his race. He was committed not only to his tennis, but also to making appearances and activities wherever he felt he could serve as an advocate for social change.

Ashe continued his impressive rise in the tennis world, winning the U.S. clay court championships in 1967, and many victories for the U. S. Davis Cup team. He had graduated from UCLA and signed on for two years in the Army. After he was commissioned, Ashe was assigned to West Point as a data processing officer and assistant tennis coach. It was hard to juggle his Army duties at West Point with a tennis career, but Ashe continued playing and winning.

In 1968, Ashe began to become more open and active on the issue of race and segregation. He gave a speech at a church in Washington D.C. about segregation and quickly found himself reprimanded by his superiors. As a legal representative of the Army, he found he was not allowed to speak out on social issues. Characteristically, Ashe channeled his frustration into his game. Excellence would be his weapon of choice against claims of racial inferiority.

Two events during this time period moved him deeply. In April of that year, civil rights leader Martin Luther King was assassinated. Then, only two months later, another leading advocate for civil rights, Robert Kennedy was assassinated. Ashe felt even more keenly the need to show the world that an African American man could succeed in the white world of tennis.

He launched one of the most successful periods of his tennis career. That summer Ashe won the men's singles title at the U.S. national championships in Brookline, Massachusetts, and then entered the prestigious U.S. Open. It was the first time the U.S. championship tournament was open to professional players as well as amateurs, making it especially challenging. Ashe was at his peak. He went on to win the tournament—the first black male to win what was by far the most prestigious tennis tournament in the United States, and perhaps the world.

Over the next several years, Ashe continued to play at top levels. He won the Australian Open singles title, and doubles titles at the French Open and Australian Open. He continued to play on the United States Davis Cup team, serving 11 times between 1963 and 1978, and compiling a singles record of 27 wins and only 5 losses. In 1975, in the match that may have been the most famous of his career, he beat Jimmy Connors to win the Wimbledon championship, and achieved the ranking of number one tennis player in the world.

Throughout all of this time, tennis was not Ashe's only commitment. He continued to be concerned with issues of social justice. After leaving the Army he began to speak out more forcefully. In 1968, following his win at the U.S. Open, he became the first athlete ever to appear on the CBS television show Face the Nation, where he talked about rising momentum among black athletes as a result of the recent civil rights legislation. A year later, he applied for a visa to play in South Africa as the number one ranked American. When the visa was denied because of his race, he made headlines by calling for the expulsion of South Africa from the International Lawn Tennis Federation. Four years later, in 1973, South Africa finally granted him a visa as they tried to improve their image in advance of hosting the 1976 Olympics. Ashe again spoke forcefully. He refused to be one of those famous blacks who were admitted as an "honorary white," and then were allowed to play only in front of all-white audiences. As a condition of accepting the visa, Ashe insisted that the audiences not be racially segregated, and that he be allowed to travel and talk freely. Because of his international stature as a player, South Africa accepted his terms.

Ashe's win in 1975 at Wimbledon put him at the top of his game. He was ranked as the number one male tennis player in the world, and was the first black athlete to win both Wimbledon and the U.S. Open. Sponsors were eager to sign him up and he drew large crowds wherever he went. Exhibition fees doubled, and so did the demands for appearances and speaking skills. He won five more tournaments in 1976, and was widely in demand as a speaker.

He seemed on top of the world, but things only got better when the brightest event in his life materialized in the form of an intelligent, articulate, sensitive, and pretty photographer and graphic artist named Jeanne Moutoussamy. Of African American and East Indian heritage, Jeanne worked for an NBC television station and was assigned to photograph Ashe at a fund raising program for the United Negro College Fund. He was immediately attracted to her, and she to him. She bore a striking resemblance to his mother — so much so that his father was shocked by the resemblance when he met Jeanne for the first time. Ashe himself recounted that he felt the resemblance of Jeanne to his mother helped to bring them together. He often enjoyed surprising Jeanne with a red rose, just as his father had done so many years ago for *his* wife.

Arthur and Jeanne were married in 1977 by Ashe's close friend Andrew Young, U. S. Ambassador to the United Nations. Ashe was on crutches for the wedding, a result of an operation to remove a bone spur from his heel. It seemed strange to see this young and vital athlete looking so vulnerable at his wedding but in some ways it was an omen of things to come. After the wedding Ashe was plagued with minor injuries that took their toll on his game. He was happier than he had ever been in his personal life but his professional life began to slip. By 1979 he failed to qualify for the Grand Prix Masters. Sponsorships began to fade, and his game suffered from his injuries and his attention to the other dimensions of his life. He was still well regarded and widely respected: Success on the tennis court had allowed him a platform to be both a role model, and a spokesperson for justice and social change. He began to think about retiring from tennis and using his talent and skills in other ways.

His Body Lets Him Down

Change was about to be forced upon Ashe. In 1979, after conducting a clinic for underprivileged children in New York City he suffered a heart attack. He was only thirty-six years old, when he was told by his doctors that he would need an operation or his tennis career would be over. He underwent quadruple bypass surgery a few months later with the hope that he would soon be able to play tennis again. He had enjoyed a wonderful career and did not want it to end. After the surgery and recovery he began a series of exercises to regain his strength.

180

While on a visit to Cairo in March 1980 with his wife, he went for a jog. It was three months after surgery, and Ashe felt completely recovered and almost ready to return to professional tennis. But shortly into his run, he was struck by a sharp pain in his chest, "It hit me relatively softly, but hard enough to stop me dead in my tracks. I felt the world come to a halt. I walked slowly back to the hotel."[12]

After seeing a doctor, Ashe knew his competitive tennis career was over. His heart had suffered damage that could not be fully remedied. On the way home from Cairo, he and Jeanne stopped in Amsterdam. Visiting an art gallery he loved, he found his attention riveted to a particular painting. It was named *The Prophet Jeremiah Lamenting the Destruction of Jerusalem*. He said to wife Jeanne that in the painting, Jeremiah looked like "he is not entirely resigned to the destruction of Jerusalem. He is taking it pretty hard. In fact, I see a hint of disgust in his face . . . I know exactly how he feels."[13]

Retirement

The loss of his tennis career was very hard on Arthur Ashe. He described his ill-fated jog when the angina occurred as "the collapse of my dreams of returning in glory to the tennis courts . . . one life had ended, and another had not yet begun. For some years I had known this year would come, but now it was here in earnest."[14] The athlete was now faced with the reality of transitioning to a new kind of life.

Back at home, he wrote a letter to 22 friends and acquaintances that he was retiring from competitive tennis, and later confirmed his retirement to the press in New York City. The transition to retirement was far more difficult than

Ashe would have imagined. "It seemed to me quite possibly a developing crisis. I felt a subtle but pervasive dissatisfaction with my life up to that point, and a deep confusion about the rest of it would, and should, look like."[15]

Ashe knew that objectively it didn't make any sense to feel that way. He knew he had lived what many would say was a dream-life. He had international fame, he traveled the world, he had made a great deal of money, he had many friends. He felt he had no right to be dissatisfied — but he was.

Ashe knew that such a transition is hard for all athletes. He saw retirement as part of a natural sequence of events for most people, when body and mind are both slowing down with age. But for athletes, he felt that their relatively young, forced retirement was an "unnatural rite, a feared and unwelcome event" for which most were totally unprepared.[16] He knew from his own experience with athletes that "the sudden darkness of retirement is for some professional athletes, including tennis players, a shock to the nervous system from which they never completely recover."[17]

Ashe viewed himself as cautious and reflective, and had thought about such matters more than most athletes, but even he felt totally unprepared for the ending of his competitive career. He worried about how he'd react to losing the glitter and the glamour, the pampering and the privilege. "Would I end up like so many other ex-athletes ... haunting bars and picking up women, or loafing in my 'den,' swilling beer and playing videocassettes of the highlights of my career over and over. . . That was not what I wanted."[18]

Although his competitive tennis career was over, Ashe had many opportunities to continue involvement in the sport. Looking for different retirement options, it was appealing to consider some of these opportunities. He became a commentator for ABC Sports and HBO Sports, and a regular columnist for *Tennis Magazine* and the *Washington Post*. And most importantly, he became the non-playing captain of the U.S. Davis Cup Team in 1980, responsible for player selection and team management. He immersed himself in that challenge as seriously as he had every other test of his life.

Being captain of the Davis Cup team was a challenge for Ashe. It brought him into supervisory contact with John McEnroe—the resident "bad boy" of the tennis circuit. A brilliant player with a foul mouth and wild temper, McEnroe was the exact temperamental opposite of Arthur Ashe. It was stressful and demanding for Ashe to captain a team with McEnroe as the central star. McEnroe thrived on conflict and strident behavior as much as Ashe abhorred it. At one point it got so bad that Ashe asked U. S. Davis cup officials to back him as he planned to forfeit a match the next time McEnroe acted up. Ashe had great respect for McEnroe's talent, but no respect at all for the way he conducted himself on the court.

In *Days of Grace,* Ashe recalls the Davis Cup finals match when McEnroe's failure to curb his obscene language drove Ashe to the brink of physical violence. McEnroe had lost his temper several times and yelled at both the crowd and his opponents, who continued to goad him. Ashe continued to try to calm down his players and went out to talk to McEnroe.

> "This is a disgrace. You cannot continue like this. I do not want to hear another obscenity out here. You are playing for the United States. Remember that!"
> I thought I saw John pull himself together, but then as he walked onto the court [his opponent] looked at him sweetly and lisped, provocatively, "you're so nice!"

"Go fuck yourself!" McEnroe screamed.

I was stunned. I stormed onto the court and John and I exchanged some bitter words for a few seconds. This time I thought I might punch John. I have never punched anyone in my life, but I was truly on the brink of hitting him. I had never been so angry in my life. I couldn't trust myself not to strangle him. Of course, if I had, any jury would have acquitted me.[19]

Ashe had a wonderful capacity to remain objective. He saw complicated issues in their full light. Strong as his feelings were against McEnroe's objectionable behavior, he complimented McEnroe as "the kind of tennis player the world might only see every 50 years" and "probably the best doubles player who had ever lived."[20]

Reflecting later on his complex feelings about McEnroe, Ashe wondered whether he may have sensed that in some ways McEnroe reflected a part of himself that he had always suppressed:

I suspect now that McEnroe and I were not so far apart after all. Far from seeing John as an alien, I think I may have known him, probably without being fully aware of my feeling, as a reflection of an intimate part of myself. This sense of McEnroe as embodying feelings I could only repress, or as a darker angle to my tightly restrained spirit, may explain why I always hesitated to interfere with his rages. . . . Now I wonder whether I had not always been aware, at some level, that John was expressing my own rage, my own anger, for me, as I could never express it.[21]

The David Cup team was not as successful as many had hoped. In 1985 Arthur Ashe was fired as captain of the team. The team was not winning and that issue was the expressed reason for his losing the position, but his active involvement in social issues and his strong opposition to apartheid may also have also played a role. Ashe was a self-described loner: "My setbacks with the Davis Cup helped me to understand that to be effective, I would have to step more boldly into the spotlight, especially if I wished to be effective in the crucial area of social and political progress."[22]

He had felt fortunate to have his captaincy in the Davis Cup serve as a bridge into retirement from competitive tennis. At first the firing was a shock, but Ashe soon came to see it in a broader perspective. It freed him from the concerns of professional tennis, and allowed him to turn his full attention toward other matters of personal significance. More and more his black roots became central in his definitional search:

> I am an African American, one born in the iron grip of legal segregation. Aside from my feelings about religion and family, my innermost stirrings have to do with trying to overcome racism and other forms of social injustice, with a search for dignity and power in a world so often hostile to us. Not the tennis court, but the arena of protest and politics would be the single most important testing ground for me in the middle years of my life.[23]

For Ashe, tennis success had never been the most important mission in his life. He was a complex and well-educated individual with a strong social conscience, who was in the process of turning away from success and toward significance for this new stage of his life.

Making the transition from star athlete to social activist, in the years following his retirement from competitive tennis, was especially challenging for Ashe. He had always had an intense need to feel he could make a moral difference in the world, to achieve something in life beyond the tennis court. He felt few people took professional athletes seriously, and he wanted to be taken seriously.

Ashe admired other black athletes who had stood up against racism and "insisted on being heard ... on weighty matters of civil rights and social responsibility and the destiny of black Americans in the modern world."[24] He worried that "[I] had not done as much as I should have in the arena of protest and politics, civil rights, and social reform."[25] Now, with less need for caution and his tennis career over, he felt driven to do more.

After the end of his competitive tennis career he had embarked on a period of soul searching. For a period of time he sought the services of a psychiatrist to help him sort through why he felt this acute sense of "emptiness." His wife Jeanne, sensitive to what he was going through, gave him Daniel J. Levison's book *Seasons of a Man's Life*, which he found profound and fascinating. He was particularly attracted by Levison's idea that a man seeks a "culminating event" in his life. From an outsider's point of view this might have been his win at Wimbledon, but Ashe felt differently. "My 'culminating event' could never be physical, never something athletic."[26] He knew that for him it would have to relate to achieving some higher goal.

Through this searching Ashe had become clear about what he wanted to do with his life. He combined a continuing active involvement in tennis, which maintained his high profile, with a strong commitment to a set of social causes like civil rights, the struggle against apartheid, and the effort of black athletes struggling to overcome racism. He taught an honors seminar on the modern black athlete at a small Florida college. He founded numerous charitable organizations including the

Arthur Ashe Institute for Urban Health, the Athletes-Career Connection, The Safe Passage Foundation, The ADC Cities Tennis Program, and the National Junior Tennis League. He also served as chairman of the American Heart Association.

During this period of time, while preparing to teach his course about black athletes, he found that writings on the history of sports had a remarkable lack of information about black athletes. He turned his energy to writing *A Hard Road to Glory,* an impressive three-volume history of black athletes that was the most comprehensive work on the subject ever published. He was so committed to the project that he spent $300,000 of his own money to research and write this well respected book.[27] *A Hard Road to Glory* was published in 1988. It continues to be one of the staples on the shelves of most libraries.

Ashe was continuing to find his way into arenas of social concern that were most important to him. He had befriended black South African leader Nelson Mandela, and became an active opponent of apartheid. Because of his active involvement, he was arrested in 1985 during an anti-apartheid protest in Washington D.C. Later that year he demonstrated against apartheid at the United Nations in New York City. "Marching in a protest is a liberating experience," he said. "It's cathartic."[28]

Arthur Ashe had suffered medical setbacks that had forced him to retire before he was ready, but he was certainly not loafing on the coach replaying video highlights of his tennis career. He was living a rich and colorful life and at the same time finding serious meaning in a host of social causes he felt were worthwhile. After reorganizing his priorities following the Davis Cup firing he was finally doing what he truly wanted to do—and what he felt was important to do. He was enjoying his life and he felt he was contributing to society.

There was only one thing that could make Ashe's life better, and it happened on December 21, 1986—his daughter Camera was born. Ashe said he was completely surprised how much he would love fatherhood. He loved helping his daughter, teaching her, protecting her, and most of all loving her. He had made an admirable transition into retirement, terminating his tennis career and launching a significant new phase of his life.

More Bad Luck

No matter how carefully you plan your life or how honorably you conduct it, you are never immune to the ravages of chance. No matter how well you live your life, you can be laid low by a string of bad luck.

Arthur Ashe had known his share of bad luck with his health. He had various minor ailments while playing professional tennis—injuries, eye infections, heel spurs that led to operations on his feet—not enough to terminate his career, but enough to interrupt it. Then came his heart attack in 1979; a quadruple-bypass surgery five months later; renewed heart problems that led to another open heart surgery in 1983; and continued problems with his heart and circulatory system.

There had been other family tragedies as well. Jeanne's father had suffered a major heart attack in 1974; her sister underwent open heart surgery in 1978; her father was hospitalized for angina in 1979; and, most devastating, Jeanne's brother died of a heart attack in 1982 at the age of 39. The emotional toll of these events must have been enormous.

But the worst was yet to come. In August 1988, Ashe began to feel a numbness in his hand that got worse and worse. It was diagnosed as resulting from a brain tumor, and he had brain surgery the next month. The tumor turned out to be a kind that often resulted from AIDS. Blood testing confirmed the fact: Arthur Ashe had AIDS.

The cause was clear. Ashe's second open-heart surgery had been more difficult than the first. He came out of the operation weak and anemic. Ashe agreed to receive two units of blood to help with his recovery from the surgery. It was later discovered that the blood was contaminated with the HIV virus, and while the blood did speed his recovery, it set in motion his descent into AIDS. Had the operation occurred two years later, routine testing of donor blood for AIDS would have prevented such a terrible consequence. It was consummate bad luck!

Ashe and his wife Jeanne decided to keep his condition private. They knew the disease was widely feared and viewed as a social stigma. For Ashe, with his great concern for his reputation, it must have been especially frustrating that there would be no way to prevent rumors and speculation about how he might have contracted the disease. At this time, AIDS was seen as an affliction of promiscuous gay men. Additionally, he had no good rhetorical options. If he denied the rumors, he would look guilty; if he said nothing, he would also look guilty.

Ashe also realized that announcing he had AIDS might jeopardize the contracts he had for endorsements, his consulting fees, and his ability to travel internationally. Ashe did contact the companies he had contracts with and inform them privately, so they could withdraw their contracts if they chose. But beyond that, Ashe and his wife felt this was a private matter and should be nobody's concern but their own.

Despite his disease, Ashe continued his commitment to social causes. The illness made him more determined than ever to dedicate his time and energy to the causes and activities that were meaningful and significant to him. He continued his interest in studying and writing about black athletes and their struggle for equality, on the playing fields and off; he continued his frequent speaking engagements; he promoted tennis for the young in urban areas; and he dedicated large amounts of time to his family, both immediate and extended.

Forced to Go Public

One day a good friend who worked at **USA Today** asked to talk to him. The newspaper had heard that Ashe had AIDS and the editor wanted to know if it was true. Ashe wouldn't lie. He refused to either confirm or deny the story. He called the editor of the paper and argued strenuously that his health was nobody's concern but his own, maintaining that he'd announced his retirement in 1980, and that he was no longer a public figure.

But the editor wouldn't budge, insisting that Ashe *was* a public figure, and that the public had a right to know. **USA Today** wanted to publish the story, and in fact, the editor already was acting with some restraint. They wouldn't publish the story until the facts could be confirmed. Still, Ashe knew they were hot on the story and soon would get some kind of confirmation—he had to act fast.

Ashe and Jeanne had feared this day might come. They had worried and agonized over how to handle the threat of public exposure. They thought it was completely unfair that Ashe's condition should be made public and they knew it would forever change their lives. Now the issue was at hand and they were forced to respond.

Ashe immediately canceled all his appointments and began plans for a news conference the next day. With the pressure that the paper was soon to make this issue public, Ashe crafted his own statement with the help of his good friend and co-author Frank Deford.

The next day Ashe held a press conference, expecting a small group of reporters would show up. Instead, the room was packed with reporters, and a podium was cluttered with microphones. Ashe had an entourage with him that included friends, his AIDS physician Dr. Stephen Scheidt, and his wife Jeanne.

He opened his remarks with a joke about George Steinbrenner's management of the Yankees, but no one laughed. This was a serious issue and a big story for the media. Everyone knew why they were there, and levity was not part of the agenda. Ashe then related the story of his heart operations and how he eventually contracted HIV from a transfusion during the second open heart surgery. He described his brain surgery in 1988, the discovery that he had AIDS, and the realization that the transfusions he had been given in the 1983 operation had most likely been contaminated.

He felt an obligation to defend his reluctance to go public with this information. He explained that this all was a deeply personal matter and that there were several reasons he felt it was legitimate to keep his situation private. When he began to talk about his wife and daughter, Camera, he was overwhelmed with emotion. Tears came to his eyes and words began to fail him. After a long silence Ashe turned his text over to Jeanne who finished reading it for him. In his statement, Ashe said that **USA Today** had put him in the unenviable position of having to lie if he wanted to protect his privacy. He felt no one should have to make that choice. He also stated in the transcript that both Jeanne and Camera were in excellent health and had tested negative for HIV. He reaffirmed that he would continue to support the causes that he had been associated with, as well as AIDS activism. Then for about 45 minutes he took a bevy of questions. Ashe said he had no plans to sue the hospital where he received the HIV-infected blood, because he did not blame anyone. To the question "Do you feel forced out?" he responded "Absolutely. If the person hadn't called the newspaper, I'd still be living a normal life."[29]

Some of Ashe's friends had told him he would feel relived once his disease was made public. He himself had thought it might be like walking out of the confessional booth at the Catholic Church and feeling like a burden had been lifted. But he decided this analogy was wrong. There was nothing he should feel guilty about. He had been made to feel guilty — but had done nothing wrong. His experience brought home to him just how strong the social stigma of AIDS was. He described the illness as the most feared disease since the Black Plague.

Talking about all this in public had the effect of emphasizing the terminal nature of his illness. While Ashe preferred to be hopeful about his condition, he could not help but notice that others had started to talk about him in the past tense. One sports writer wrote about this directly:

> People talk about beating cancer. No one talks about beating AIDS. . . . It began for Arthur Ashe on Wednesday. Testimonials. Tributes. Words on a Tombstone. He was a great champion. He

battled apartheid, he spoke eloquently on black issues, he was a fine man. All in the past tense. He *was*.[30]

It was deep in Ashe's character and nature to be positive and optimistic about all things in his life. It was, indeed, these qualities that had made him a champion. But now with AIDS as part of his social and emotional structure, Ashe was faced with the difficult challenge of remaining optimistic about a condition for which the general public felt no optimism. Most people were frightened of the condition and suspicious of all those who had it.

Even harder than explaining his situation to the press was explaining it to his five year old daughter, Camera. He and Jeanne knew that Camera would be exposed to comments by schoolmates and friends, and some of those comments might be insensitive and hurtful. This issue was one of the forces driving Ashe's desire for privacy with respect to the condition of AIDS. In *Days of Grace* Ashe describes telling Camera about his condition. It was several months after the press conference and Arthur and Jeanne had a sense that comments were getting back to Camera. One Sunday as she was drifting to sleep she opened her eyes and asked her father:

> "Daddy, how did you get AIDS?"
> I shuddered. I hadn't expected the question at all, certainly not now, not dredged up, as it were, from her subconscious, where it obviously had been stirring awhile. . . .
> "Well," I told her. "It was like this. I was in the hospital. I had to have an operation. During the operation, you can lose a lot of blood. And after the operation, to feel better, I got a blood transfusion to replace some of the blood I had lost. I was given blood that somebody had given to the hospital for people like me. The blood turned out to be bad"

"And the person had AIDS?"

"Yes."

Camera said nothing for a moment. Then she spoke again. "Are you sure?"

"Yes Camera, I'm sure. That's how I got it." Her eyes remained open for a moment or two, and then she faded to sleep.[31]

Dedicated to the End

Faced with his own mortality, Ashe responded as he had responded to the other challenges in his past. He rededicated himself to the things that were most important in his life: his family, his friends, and his causes. While remaining active in the issues he was already committed to, Ashe added a new one—AIDS.

Ashe founded the Arthur Ashe Foundation for the Defeat of AIDS in 1992, and became a national spokesperson for the cause of battling AIDS. He spoke widely at fund raising events and other gatherings. Two months before his death he spoke at the United Nations asking delegates to increase funding for AIDS research. He felt it was important to raise the world's consciousness about this terrible disease.

But Ashe's primary commitment continued to be his work to elevate the status and freedom of black people around the globe. When asked about his feelings relating to the disadvantage of accidentally contracting AIDS Ashe would often respond that AIDS paled in comparison to the challenge of being born and raised black. He continued to work for the causes of racial and social equality for his entire life, and even beyond, in his posthumously published memoir. In 1992, just a few months before his death, he was arrested outside

194

the White House in a protest against American treatment of Haitian refugees.

His final memoir, ***Days of Grace,*** was finished just prior to his death. It was his last effort to leave a statement about many of the causes he believed in—and perhaps even a legacy of hope for all those who cope with this dreaded disease. Like Ashe himself, the book is optimistic and positive, always filled with hope, never with anger or bitterness. Ashe himself did not choose the book's title—his editor did after his death—but the title is an appropriate expression of Ashe's style. In a world filled with anger and confrontation, Ashe was recognized as a beacon of style and grace.

Ashe's overarching quality was his optimism. It was remarkable in all ways. As he told a reporter shortly before his death: "I have so much to be thankful for. For someone with AIDS, as with any life-threatening illness, the family is often a bulwark against embittering anxiety and the darkest depression. On every side my family supports me."[32] Even as his health declined Ashe had little time for self-pity. He told a writer, "if I ask 'why me?' about my troubles, I would have to ask 'why me' about my blessings. Why my winning Wimbledon? Why me marrying a beautiful, gifted woman, and having a wonderful child?"[33]

Recognitions began to flow toward Ashe as he struggled to constructively live out the final chapter of his life. He received the Helen Hayes Award, the National Urban League Award, the first annual AIDS Leadership Award of the Harvard AIDS Institute, the American Sportscasters Association Sports Legend Award, and the Sportsman of the Year award by the editors of ***Sports Illustrated*** magazine.

Ashe's race against time ended February 6, 1993. He was hospitalized with a deadly pneumonia virus that attacks many AIDS sufferers. He died quickly of complications resulting from the virus, the pneumonia, and his general weakened condition.

More than 11,000 people attended his memorial services in New York and in his hometown of Richmond, where he was buried. Jesse Jackson and other noted speakers delivered eulogies praising his dignity, character, and his dedicated work for the social causes he believed in. Ashe's friend, sportswriter Frank Deford, was eloquent in his praise:

> In the end, the outpouring of emotion we gave to him spoke selfishly to our hope — that if we could not save his life, what he stood for might help to save us. . . . He was, I came to think, in matters of race, the Universal Soldier, some kind of keystone figure we need if ever brothership is to triumph.[34]

What the Arthur Ashe Story Tells Us

Health Matters

In previous chapters we have talked about various ways to prepare for retirement and to make retirement better. But as we have discussed, there are two huge things we may not have much control over. One is health, and the other is luck. We can do some preparation, we can do some planning for possible—or even inevitable—physical decline, but we simply can't fully control what is going to happen to us.

When our health is good we hardly think about it; when it is bad, it can dominate our life. The Arthur Ashe story is one in which physical health played an enormous role. First, his heart attack forced his premature retirement from tennis. Then a tainted blood transfusion gave him AIDS, forcing him to fight for his very life. Ironically Ashe, who valued his reputation above all else, had contracted the one disease that, rather than engendering sympathy, often makes people question one's character. The way he responded to those challenges offers insights for all of us.

Arthur Ashe was more aware than most of us that his body would someday let him down. As an athlete he knew his career in sports would end early and he would have to restructure his life around some new endeavor. The little aches and pains that most of us can ignore were for him an early sign of the physical decline he knew would necessarily come. But he was not prepared for it to come as soon as it did. When heart problems did lead him to retire from tennis, he faced this forced early retirement with a positive attitude. Knowing

197

others who had not reacted well when they were forced out of their sports career, Ashe was determined to handle this transition in a positive way. He knew he was embarking on a "second career" and had every reason to hope would last many more years. He thought carefully about what he wanted to do with his life, and he made the decision to embark on a life committed to the social causes he believed in.

When Ashe faced a new health challenge only a few years later, with his discovery that he had AIDS, it must have been devastating. Although heart problems ran in his family, he had no reason to suspect he would be brought down by a blood transfusion that gave him an incurable and fatal disease. For most people this news would be emotionally and psychologically overwhelming, but Ashe faced the situation with courage and elegance. He never let it overwhelm him or turn him from his goals. He also never let it make him into the kind of person he did not want to be. His story illustrates perhaps the best one could do in a situation like the one he faced.

The Arthur Ashe story raises the broader question of the impact of health on retirement. Sooner or later, almost all of us will face health challenges. They may come early and lead to a retirement before we had planned, or they may come later, well after we have retired. They may be sudden and unexpected, or they may more subtle and gradual, an accumulation of small problems, aches, and pains that drain us and leave us with less energy. Ashe's story illustrates that we can never fully plan for what might happen to our health, but it also brings into focus some things we can do. Although we can't fully control our health, there are some things we can control. Some of these relate to practical considerations; some of them relate to our mental framework and our attitude.

When health problems begin, or when advancing age makes it sensible to consider preparation for declining health, it is sometimes hard to make ourselves face this fact and make good practical decisions. Ashe was always careful and methodical about his health. When he had his angina attack in Cairo, he knew it made sense to return home to where he could obtain good medical care, and he immediately did so. When AIDS began to take its toll, he and his family moved back into New York City so he could be near a hospital he trusted. The thing that Ashe did that was so impressive was to quickly face each new situation and make a sensible decision about what needed to be done.

Many of us will need to make decisions related to our health. Some of these will be major, such as when we need to move to a retirement community or to a health care facility, proximity to medical care, necessity for special living arrangements, or the need for special assistance. Others will be seemingly minor, like knowing when it is time to add extra safety precautions like a railing on the steps or a grab bar in the shower. Even something as simple as seeking medical advice when symptoms occur is sometimes hard to do. It is easy to postpone these decisions or ignore signs of increasing needs. It would be wise to think of Ashe as a role model, with his remarkable ability to simply accept the changed situation and decide to make sensible choices about what needed to be done next.

There are some things about our health we can control. Everyone today should take it upon themselves to become knowledgeable about the powerful importance of diet, nutrition, and exercise in terms of susceptibility to disease. Everyone should be aware of the enormous effect that obesity, alcohol, and smoking have on health. Arthur Ashe was very aware of his family history of heart disease. While he could not eliminate that genetic effect, he did do everything in his power to postpone its effect — eating carefully, maintaining his weight, and avoiding smoking or excessive drinking, not only while he was an athlete, but after his athletic career ended.

Luck Figures into the Equation

We live in a modern world that sometimes fools us into believing that most of life is controllable. Then, every once in a while, something reminds us that there are many things in life that are not within our control, and that our only choice is to make the "best of a bad situation."

We can agree with the old adage that it is important to accept the things you can't change and have the courage to change those things you can change. We should work hard to make things better but at the same time we need to recognize that certain things are not going to change and we need to accept them as they are. The very difficult challenge is to evaluate thoughtfully what we can change and what can not.

Often people faced with some malady or tragedy think they can't do anything about the situation and give up, only to realize later that others faced with the same problem were able to take some positive action to deal with it. Still, having said that, many of us live with an unvoiced fear that one day we will get some bad news about something we cannot change, something that will be difficult to accept, even for the most optimistic personality. Ashe was remarkable in this sense. He passed quickly into the zone of acceptance of each new situation and thus was able to maximize the opportunities he had.

Much has been written by writers like Martin Seligman and Rabbi Harold Kushner about maintaining a positive attitude and coping with life when "bad things happen to good people." These two ideas seem to coalesce at the point when our only way to remain positive about our lives, in the face of severe adversity, is to accept what is spread out before us as our destiny and continue to attempt to live the best life we have the ability to live, given the situation, time, and resources we have left. It is at this point that the struggle for change must be transformed into the struggle for acceptance — the only realistic option left. Many are not able to make this transformation. A rare few accomplish it with such grace and dignity as to become an archetype for what is possible.

Arthur Ashe was such a person. First, Ashe had the bad luck of being a supreme athlete whose body let him down with a young-life heart condition that forced him out of the game he loved. Then came the colossal bad luck of contracting AIDS through a blood transfusion following his second heart operation. That would surely plunge most people into a sea of "why me" self-pity and sense of unfairness at having this curse delivered to them, when they played no role to deserve it. As a black man in a white dominated world, Ashe knew unfairness all his life. He fought against it and struggled not to allow that unfairness to define him. Like the biblical Job, it began to seem that his destiny was to endure more than many others and more than seemed fair, well beyond measure. Who would criticize him if he treated himself to some bitterness and righteous indignation? But that is not the path Ashe chose.

Possibly because of his masterful control of the unfairness presented to him all his life, Ashe quietly and with dignity and humility, set about controlling those things he could control, and accepting that which was beyond his control. He did this so well, in fact, that many who interviewed him found it hard to believe he was not bitter. But he would calmly assert that his life was not in fact full of bad luck but good luck. His career, his family, his child, his wife, his success, and his achievements were all tempered by good luck: good luck that far outweighed the bad luck of getting AIDS. He seemed genuine in his acceptance of his condition and his resolve to live what life he had left to the fullest extent possible—without the resentment and anger to which many would feel entitled.

Arthur Ashe's last life chapters are inspirational and exceptional. He reexamined his life, redirecting his energy toward his family and socially worthy causes. In doing so he made his bad luck almost look enviable. But with deeper inspection we realize that what is truly enviable here is that he finished his life the way we all wish we could—living and loving to his fullest potential right to the end. His story and his example should not be forgotten.

Character Counts

What Ashe's story shows us is that there is one thing you can control when health declines—and that is how you cope with your loss. Ashe showed that character counts. It is possible to take great adversity, and respond to it without letting it devastate you or turn you into the kind of person you do not want to be. One of the most impressive things about Arthur Ashe is that he never riled against the unfairness of what happened to him. Some parents tell their children: "life is just unfair so you'd better get used to it," but in fact, most of us *don't* get used to it. Most of us either get angry, or feel sorry for ourselves—or both. Ashe seems to have avoided both of these reactions.

For Ashe, part of his ability to respond so well to adversity may have stemmed from the fact that adversity was not new to him. Sports, in the best sense, may have served him well. In the sports world, he was forced to face defeat and loss, and had more practice dealing with it than most people.

But even beyond his sports experiences, Ashe's ability to cope with adversity may have been forged in his having to do that all his life—as an African American growing up in a segregated society. A statement he made near the end of his life was revealing. It was after an hour-long interview with a reporter from *People* magazine about how he was coping with AIDS. The reporter said to Ashe, "I guess this must be the heaviest burden you ever had to bear, isn't it?" He replied: "No, it isn't." He went on to explain:

> . . . being black is the greatest burden I have had to bear . . . race has always been my biggest burden. Having to live as a minority in America, even now it continues to feel like an extra weight tied around me. . . . Race is for me a more onerous burden than AIDS. My disease is the result of biological factors, over which we have no control. Racism, however, is entirely made by people, and therefore, it hurts and inconveniences infinitely more."[35]

In his autobiography, he said that he knew he had a wonderful life, he felt proud of himself and proud to be an African American. He knew he was self confident and self assured, as one would have to be to be as successful as he had been as an athlete. But the segregation he experienced as a youth, and the racism present in subtle and not-so-subtle ways throughout his life, "left me a marked man, forever aware of a shadow of contempt that lays across my identity and my sense of self esteem. . . . The mere memory of it darkens my most sunny days. . . . The shadow is always there; only death will free me and blacks like me from its pall."[36]

In the final chapter of Ashe's autobiography, he gives some advice to his daughter Camera. He explains that she will undoubtedly experience racism and sexism in her life, but she must always resist the temptation to despair. "Racism and sexism must never be an excuse for not doing your best. Racism and sexism will probably always exist, but you must always try to rise above them."[37]

Ashe's advice certainly captures what he himself did throughout his life. He never let his health problems overwhelm him, never let himself rile in anger against his fate, never let himself abandon his commitment to continuing his social activism. He never let himself become a bitter person, never let himself become so angry or discouraged that he stopped being the kind of supportive parent and positive person that he wanted to be. And, if he felt despair, it was never for long. Like the Delany sisters, his strong character may have arisen from the adversity he felt growing up under segregation, coupled with a strong family that offered support and moral guidance. Early on, he made an inner decision that he would not let adversity turn him into someone negative or cynical, but rather he would use it to help him become a stronger person.

Our Talk Matters: Attitude Makes a Difference

Arthur Ashe faced much he could not control near the end of his life, but the one thing he could control was his attitude. Like Ashe, many of us may face some adversity over which we have no control, but all of us do have some control over how we respond to that adversity. Much of this control comes from how we talk about it, both to ourselves and to others. Again, as we have seen before, the talk matters. Our self-talk has a powerful influence on how we frame things and how we respond to them.

Elizabeth Kübler-Ross argued that people facing death often go through a series of stages. She described them as denial, anger, bargaining, depression, and finally acceptance. Indeed, these stages of reaction may be experienced by people following a broad variety of unexpected losses: a divorce, death of a loved one, personal health problems, or even a career failure. But there is considerable variability from person to person in how they experience these stages and indeed whether they experience them at all. Not all individuals go through all of these reactions, and different people experience different reactions in different strengths and perhaps in a different sequence. To a considerable extent, our reactions derive from our attitudes, and our attitudes derive from our language.

When health problems strike, we can focus on our losses and worry about future losses. Or, we can follow Ashe's example and try to force ourselves to look at things differently, to reframe the situation, to talk to ourselves in a different way. We can look at the abilities we still have. We can explicitly make comparisons to those who have less, and remind ourselves of our blessings. This is an approach that one author has described as one of the routes to enhanced happiness and life satisfaction.[38] We can focus on relationships that still exist, experiences we still have, positive memories. We can discover ways to get enjoyment from our daily lives despite physical limitations.

Such re-framing may come naturally to us out of our past experiences. Perhaps, as with Arthur Ashe, we may have past experiences with adversity that help us. Or we may make a conscious decision to revise our self-talk because we realize that doing so can help us feel better about our situation. It can help us see the glass half full instead of half empty, help us feel good about what we have instead of bad about what we have lost, help us feel optimism instead of despair, and ultimately help us be the kind of person we want to be for both ourselves and those around us.

The Importance of Family and Friends

As Arthur Ashe experienced more and more health problems, one of the profound sources of support and inspiration for him was his family.

His belief in the importance of family began with strong guidance and support from his father that he felt throughout his life. For his father, family would be with you when all else might let you down. Arthur's father was devoted to his children, and all the more so after his wife (Ashe's mother) died and he became both father and mother to his children. Ashe himself discovered that when he married, and even more so when his daughter Camera arrived, his own family became far more important to him than he would have imagined. Family became in some ways the highest priority for him. Indeed, when the issue of his AIDS becoming public arose, his first and major concern was what impact that would have on his daughter Camera.

Ashe found that at the end of his life, he wasn't thinking about his glorious days of tennis, but about his daughter. It was profoundly important to him that she have good memories of him. He wanted to leave a legacy, and the legacy he wanted to leave was a statement about love and family. He thought of his own memories of his mother, regretting that he had only one image of his mother while she was still alive. It was a still image in his mind, like a snap-shot, of her standing in a doorway shortly before she died. He embarked on a project with his wife Jeanne, with Jeanne taking hundreds of photographs of Ashe and his daughter, resulting in a children's book *Daddy and Me.* He knew from his own experience that memories fade, so he wanted Camera to have something to remember him by. Something more than he himself had had, that would be permanent when memories fade.

The last chapter of Ashe's autobiography contains what Ashe believed might be his last letter to his beloved daughter Camera. The letter begins and ends talking about the importance of family. Ashe says that, ever since he was a child and saw his father lose his own father and his wife (Ashe's mother) in less than one year, "Family has meant more to me than you can imagine."[39] He describes a powerful image of the family as a tree, a tree with many branches, but also with deep roots, able to sway in the wind and survive because of those deep roots. "When you see a magnificent tree anywhere you know it has had to fight and sway and bend in order to survive. Families that survive are like that tree."[40]

Beyond his immediate family, Ashe's extended family was supportive throughout his health difficulties. He also valued the importance of friendships:

> I have invested in friendship all my life. I have been patient and attentive, forgiving and considerate, even with some people who probably did not deserve it. It did not take an enormous sacrifice, however; for whatever reason, it came almost naturally. I made the investment of time and energy and now the dividends were being returned to me in kindness. . . .[41]
>
> Traveling the world as a tennis player, I discovered that deep friendships with an infinite variety of people are not only possible, but can definitely enrich one's life beyond measure."[42]

Like Ashe, most people would say that family and friends are a most important source of joy and comfort. Many of us, in the face of the daily pressure of so many other obligations, assume our close relationships will just take care of themselves. But the fact is that often they do not. We live in a modern world where people are highly mobile, over-committed, and stressed for time. The technologies that were supposed to make our lives easier and better have, instead, increased the complexity of our lives. Modern technologies offered the promise of bringing people closer together, but all too often they have the opposite effect. For example, has television brought the American family together, or are four different people sitting in four different rooms watching four different channels? Surveys show that the one thing Americans feel most concerned about is the enormous increase in demands on their time. It is harder and harder to devote time to simply nourishing our human relationships, and they do need to be nourished. We must be on constant guard against the press of many demands that call on our time. We need to continually remind ourselves of what is really important to us.

People often feel that once they retire they will have more time to devote to family and friends. For many people this simply does not happen. They report that after retirement they feel just as busy as they did while they were working. It seems like whatever extra time they have immediately gets filled with a host of new activities and obligations. There may be other challenges to maintaining close relationships. Relationships forged at work may fade away. People move away from long-standing communities. Health conditions create new demands on our time. With age many of our activities with others become difficult to maintain.

In the face of these challenges how can we maintain our friendships and strong family ties? The first thing that needs to happen is that we must explicitly identify our relationships as a priority. But saying they are a priority is not enough. People often say family and friends are a high priority, but when asked to state specific examples of things they have done and choices they have made, they find they have done little. Ashe was a wonderful example of someone who analyzed his priorities, set goals, and had an uncanny ability to sweep away the clutter in order to act on what really mattered. Sometimes all that is needed is a firm commitment to very specific actions that will convert our stated priorities into reality.

It is important to think through what specific actions we need to take to keep our relationships from fading away. This may be a different process for men than for women. There is tendency for women to be able to maintain friendships that focus on sharing and intimacy. Men, in contrast, often need the justification of an activity to get them together. This may be harder in retirement, when previously structured activities no longer occur, or when the aging process intrudes. All this seems to make more difficult the issue of satisfactory family relationships and friendships. Ashe's advice to his daughter, in the final chapter of his book, would be good for us all to remember:

> You will often feel that you don't have enough time to do what you want to do. Make time. Control time; do not let time control you any more than it must. Balance the activity of your life. . . . Don't try to do everything. Choose carefully, and then give your all to what you choose.[43]

Spirituality and Meaning

Beyond the practical plans and preparations we can make, beyond the things we say to ourselves to reframe the situation and see things positively, and beyond the support of friends and family—there is another critical issue to consider. This is the idea of meaning and spirituality. For many people this is the major organizing concept of their lives.

The idea of spirituality and meaning-making has received only brief attention in this book so far. Although everyone has a set of beliefs about life, living, and death, many people are uncomfortable discussing or examining those beliefs. Arthur Ashe was much different. He was someone for whom these issues were very important, and he was willing to contemplate many different perspectives in his own search for meaning. He read, thought, and wrote about spirituality, living, dying, and the divine. Probably stimulated by the death of his mother when he was so young, and the seeming senselessness of that

210

tragedy, it was important to Ashe to search for meaning and understanding about the nature of life and death.

The theme of spirituality and meaning is apparent with all of the people profiled in this book. They were all searching for something more to their existence than their own personal survival. They followed very different paths in their search for meaning. Some, like the Delany sisters and Carter, found meaning in their lives based on traditional Christianity grounded in a religious faith they practiced their entire lives. For others, like Katharine Hepburn and Lee Iacocca, life's meaning seemed to be represented by the sense that their work or their art produced a basis of goodness or a legacy that somehow was larger than physical existence. There is a sense in all these people that there is something more to living and dying than mere physical existence.

In the last two chapters of Ashe's final book, completed only weeks before his death, he attempted to explain his feelings about living, religion, loving, and the divine. It is obvious that as he wrote these chapters he knew his days were numbered. His AIDS had moved into final life threatening stages and his thoughts turned toward his faith, his friends, and his family. For Ashe these were intimately connected.

Ashe felt that he always retained a belief in God. He spent his final days reading the Bible more than any other book and felt that as much as he loved reading, music, and the arts, the most important connection was a spiritual one:

> In the end, as much as I love reading and music, and although love given and received by human beings is perhaps the only sure token of God's love and God's grace, I understand that the deepest consolation comes from one's relationship to the divine.[44]

Ashe's sense of the divine had expanded beyond his early Christian roots. It drew from his past experiences with Catholicism, Buddhism, Methodism, the theologian Howard Thurman, the Reverend Jefferson Rogers, and numerous other influences. Although founded in Christianity, his faith had become more eclectic, and incorporated many components drawn from a variety of other perspectives. So well respected a thinker was Ashe on this issue that when *Life* magazine ran a feature story asking the question "Is there a God?" Ashe was one of those asked to respond. He made two points in his response. First, he believed he was "part of a continuum of life that has existed, exists, and will exist into future generations. At most I am only a ripple in this mighty river of life, I am nevertheless a part of it, and a unique part, as well." Second, he believed in a creator God, even though God's existence cannot be proven scientifically. "I know that I turn my back on God only at my peril. This I shall never do."[45]

The closing pages of Ashe's autobiography contain a moving letter to his daughter, Camera, who had just turned six, the same age Ashe was when he lost his own mother. Written less than three weeks before Ashe himself died, it was written in the full knowledge that it might be his last communication to her and he wanted to carefully set down some final thoughts for her, that she could return to later in life, for guidance about life, love, God, and faith.

He used the image of "Threads in My Hands" to represent his abiding faith in goodness and love, and how those threads are ultimately woven into his love for family, friends—and especially her. It is a powerful expression of the way in which his sense of love and the divine are interwoven into a pattern of connectedness. While never directly expressed, reading the letter gives one the sense that, for Ashe, spirituality and meaning and the divine are all intimately connected with the people of one's life. The letter is sensitive and touching. It contains advice about faith, love, friendship, God, and kindness. It is easy to see the power of his faith and forgiveness as he instructs his daughter about life and faith—a life he knows he will not be around to see.

> I may not be walking with you all the way, or even much of the way, as I walk with you now. Don't be angry with me if I am not there in person, alive and well, when you need me. I would like nothing more than to be with you always. Do not feel sorry for me if I am gone. When we were together, I loved you deeply and you gave me so much happiness I can never repay you. Camera, wherever I am when you feel sick at heart and weary of life, or when you stumble and fall and don't know if you can get up again, think of me. I will be watching and smiling and cheering you on.[46]

Ashe stands out as someone who worked diligently to understand human loss and human pain in spiritual terms. And while he never turned from the religious grounding of his childhood, it is clear that he also felt free to embrace a wide range of disparate ideas as he pieced together the mosaic belief system that guided him. It served him well. Even as he died from what many would have riled against as a clear injustice, or monstrous bad luck, there is no sense that there was anything in his heart but love, gratitude and forgiveness. He is a marvelous example of a person who managed to use his wisdom and faith to transition from fame to retirement and, then, finally to death—at a premature age—with grace and dignity. What a wonderful world it would be if we could all be a little bit more like Arthur Ashe.

LIFE AFTER WORK

7

Final Reflections

The focus of this book has been on what we call the personal side of retirement. There have been many books on financial planning, and there is no doubt that this is an important issue. However, we believe that a successful retirement depends upon far more than financial planning. In this book we have selected individuals whose stories address central themes surrounding retirement. At the end of each of those stories we have summarized the central issues and identified important questions and conclusions. It is not our intention to repeat those conclusions here.

In this final chapter we will identify some of the key points that have emerged as we have explored this topic. We do not believe that there is a single set of "rules" for successful retirement that will apply to everyone. Rather, what we will do here is identify the handful of significant ideas and issues that a thoughtful person might want to consider about retirement.

The issues discussed below flow out of the six profiles of this book, as well as ideas from other books we have read, our work with retirement focus groups, and interviews and conversations we have had with retirees and others who are about to retire. We hope that this discussion will promote thought, conversation, and reflection on your part as well.

The Challenge of Retirement

We believe retirement can be a wonderful stage of life. Shortly we will turn to some of the ways to help make it both effective and satisfying. Before turning to these, however, it is important to recognize that moving to this stage of life can be especially challenging.

Retirement Is a Major Life Transition

One of the things that surprised us when we talked with others about retirement was the number of people who claimed that this is "no big deal." Many people act as if this whole business of retirement is simple, clear, and obvious to everyone. They act as though it is a minor life change that needs little or no reflection, and will just automatically work out by itself. All one needs to do is go to the retirement party, collect the gifts, and then start a life of endless leisure.

There may be some out there for whom this is accurate. We believe, however, that for most people retirement is a significant and life-changing event, associated with anxiety, discomfort, and hidden dimensions of which they may be only dimly aware. We believe that some of those who describe retirement as simply a minor life change may be doing so to avoid confronting issues that are uncomfortable for them.

We began this book with the true story of someone who literally committed suicide over his inability to cope with the end of his productive work life. At first we found it difficult to believe that his death was really about his inability to cope with his transition to retirement. The more we explored his situation the more we were persuaded that it was, indeed, the major cause of his unhappiness. While this situation is extreme, and we do not mean to imply that it is typical, we do believe that for many people retirement is a complex, somewhat scary, uncharted life transition, that warrants a good deal of thought, discussion, and reflection. Some people will find their lives totally reorganized after retirement, others will find new challenges and opportunities, still others may actually begin to invent a "new self" in this new stage of their lives.

A Transition Is More Than a Change

We believe that in any person's life there are many periods of change, but only a few that are truly life transitions. A transition is much more than simply a change or just a turning point in a particular individual's life. Individuals have many changes throughout their lives, and even some that would be considered turning points. In our thinking, however, a transition goes beyond this because it is culturally recognized as a major life experience. In our view transitions are socially significant and socially recognized life events that have some universality within a particular culture, and a set of shared expectations defined by that culture. As one sign of this, transitions often are recognized by a defining public ceremony—such as a wedding or graduation.

In a transition, many things change at once. These changes spread across a broad array of life dimensions. Transitions often carry with them changes in the network of friends and acquaintances, in the daily activities of living, in social activities, in financial resources and obligations, in the expectations that others have of you, and even in your perception of yourself.

218

Two examples illustrate some of these components: getting married, and becoming a parent. Consider what happens when one says for the first time "I'm a married man" or "I'm a married woman" or "I'm a mother" or "I'm a father." Each of these shifts carries with it enormous changes in a whole host of practical components of daily living.

We are reminded of one of our daughters and her husband, who, when anticipating their first child, said "this really won't change our lives very much." They couldn't have been more wrong. Almost everything in their lives changed, and changed dramatically. Transitions often have widespread and unanticipated consequences.

Frederic Hudson in his book *The Adult Years: Mastering the Art of Self-Renewal* discusses the role of transitions in our lives. He says that a person's entire life can be viewed as a series of "chapters" and "transitions." He suggests that the components of a major transition usually include:

• Movement from a time of relative stability to a time of instability and uncertainty;
- Letting go of familiar roles;
- Feelings of loss;
- Shifts in our relationships and support systems;
- Feelings of emotional stress.

Some major transitions in life include the entry into adulthood, getting married or getting divorced, and having your first child. We believe that for most people the entry into retirement also has the components that make it a major life transition. Few life transitions carry with them changes as widespread as retirement: there may be changes in relationships, work, routines of daily living, marital dynamics, friends, professional connections, social support networks, family relationships, finances, health, geographic location, feelings of being productive or effective or useful or valued, and even the way you define yourself.

The Retirement "Ceremony" and What It Reveals

The ceremony surrounding a transition often reveals something about how we view that transition. For example, when we think of someone getting married we think of the wedding ceremony and what it symbolizes. The ceremony captures the hopes and dreams of the newly formed couple, puts a societal stamp of approval on the union, and publicly expresses a set of commitments, expectations, and hopes. Because the wedding ceremony is considered so significant, it has given rise to an entire support industry in our society.

The situation with retirement is very different. When we think of a retirement, we don't automatically associate it with a ceremony. Even if there is to be a ceremony, we may have only vague and inconsistent expectations about it. Indeed, even a retiree about to attend his or her own retirement ceremony may have little idea what to expect. In his article "The Unbearable Lightness of Retirement," Joel Savishinsky makes the point that we really do not have fixed rituals for this meaningful life transition.[1] He points out that the wide range of different ritual treatments is evidence of the vagueness and confusion surrounding this life change. We agree with Savishinsky. Society's general ambivalence about the concept of retirement is shown by the inconsistencies in our retirement ceremonies.

In the absence of a clear idea of what a retirement ceremony should be, our culture has drifted toward the notion of a retirement "party." There is a lot of variation in whether or not you even have a retirement party. If you do have a party, what are the core meanings and significant concepts that are to be expressed at this event? Even the very idea that we call it a "party" and not a "ceremony" is revealing. The retirement party seems on the same level as a farewell party for an employee who is leaving the company to take a job across town. We treat this like a "goodbye party," not a marker of a major life change.

Think back to a retirement party you have attended. Possibly it was a positive, supportive, and affirming event. But it is just as likely that it was mostly a negative affair: a cynical joke-fest, a string of snide remarks about the person's work life, his or her personality, or the event itself, often devoted to "roasting" the retiree. Rarely does it include an affectionate and appreciative review of the person's work life. All this was raised to the level of a cultural cliché, and captured very well in the popular 2002 film *About Schmidt*, where the retiree himself is so disillusioned with how vacuous the ceremony is, that he slips away during the festivities for a drink and a moment of quiet, private reflection.

Rituals are social constructions that help us get through major and sometimes uncomfortable life changes. They also help us in our personal transition toward defining ourselves in a new role. Unfortunately, perhaps because the whole concept of retirement has been around for only a few generations, our society has not satisfactorily developed a set of rituals that are much help in this situation. The retirement party and its surrounding events do very little to support us as we enter this complex life transition.

Retirement Can Be an Especially Difficult Transition

There are several aspects of the retirement transition that can make it more challenging than the other transitions we have discussed. In fact, in some cases, retirement may be the most challenging life transition of all. It is surely a major change from the world of working every day, feeling useful, enjoying a predictable daily structure, and having a professional role.

Retirement may differ from other transitions such as marriage, entry into a career, or starting a family in that each of those transitions involves a move into a new identity with increased social value. Almost everyone who becomes a parent feels proud to say, "I'm a mother," or "I'm a father," but we have encountered many people who do not feel comfortable saying, "I'm retired." In our society, retirement often carries negative associations instead of being seen as a socially admired change that enhances your status. For some, retirement can be a double bind in that family and friends may support the decision to retire, but once retirement has begun, the retiree finds that the wider culture seems to value and respect them less.

All the other major life transitions seem to move us "toward" something new and definable. Retirement, on the other hand, highlights what is ending. For most people, as Savishinsky suggests, there is a great feeling of vagueness and uneasiness that silently surrounds this important life step.

The decision to retire may be particularly stressful for many people because they see it as the last, big, elective transition they are likely to have any control over. In addition, for most people the decision is irrevocable. There is no going back to the job you are leaving.

A recent study supports the view of retirement as an especially challenging transition. A study reported in 2001 examined 534 married couples. It was one of the first studies to track couples through the process of retirement. The lead author of the report, Dr. Phyllis Moen, a professor of sociology and human development at Cornell University, said her research showed that the transition put significant stress on the marital relationship. A *New York Times* article describing this research said that the shift to retirement "was a period of marital strife for men and women."[2] The main finding was that retirement itself was a happy time for couples, but the transition period into retirement was a difficult and stressful time.

Even though it is a difficult transition for many, most get through it and find pathways into new possibilities. Later in this chapter, we will outline some of the many things we can do make this transition a positive one that leads us into a new stage of life that is maximally rewarding.

The Hidden Dimensions of Retirement:
Aging, Loss, and Decline

One reason retirement can be difficult is that it has hidden dimensions and meanings. It is a transition many of us don't like to talk about. It is striking how many individuals approaching retirement, or recently retired, dislike even using the word "retirement." One person we know told us, "We need to find a better word than 'retired.' It signifies a transition into nothing. This is not how I want to see myself in this stage of my life."

For many, the concept of retirement raises the specter of loss and decline. Lurking beneath the word "retirement," like a hidden demon we do not want to acknowledge, is the idea of declining health and even death. Retirement may be the defining marker between mid-life and old age. It taps our latent fear of aging, a life without meaning, and a life without relevance. Youth seems filled with multiple potentials, but aging seems to be about fading potentials. Youth seems filled with energy, but aging seems associated with less and less energy. Even when you make plans, you wonder whether you will have the health and energy to complete them.

It can be especially hard to admit that we are aging because we live in such a youth-obsessed culture. Everywhere we look, youth and beauty are celebrated. Our media hammer us incessantly with images and messages designed to encourage fantasies of power, beauty, and youth. We are bombarded daily with messages that tell us that aging means nothing but loss. The preponderance of films and TV programs celebrate values that do not age well. Americans consume enormous amounts of mass media, but with only a few exceptions, the role models offered to us by the mass media do little to make one feel valued in the later stages of life. With all the messages we receive about what our culture values, it is little wonder that entering this stage of life carries enormous trepidation.

We found it especially revealing when we began to read articles on "aging well." The images used to illustrate "successful aging" were people who were not getting wrinkles, not slowing down, and not losing energy. One article glorified a person who was still water-skiing at age 75, and another described someone still mountain climbing at 80. We suddenly realized that "aging well" in this culture really meant *not* aging. There was no sense that successful aging might involve redefining your priorities, developing wisdom, sharing your experiences with others, or just slowing down and enjoying life.

Retiring also may involve a sense of drifting and uncertainty. Some people are losing the job that was a major force in their lives, gave their day structure, and even defined them and give them an identity. The loss of structure and identity may leave them adrift with no clear sense of direction or purpose.

All of the factors we have discussed can make retirement difficult. They make it especially important to do whatever we can to make this experience a positive one.

LIFE AFTER WORK

Making Retirement Positive

If retirement is a major transition, what are some ways we can make it a positive one? Each of the preceding chapters contains some insights that arose from considering how particular individuals coped with their specific situations. We will not repeat all of those insights here, but rather, we will describe four themes that have emerged as central in considering what makes a successful retirement.

The Three R's of Retirement

The concept of achieving some sense of balance among different dimensions of one's life has come up repeatedly throughout this book. Early in our thinking about this topic, we needed some way to easily think about the important areas of life as they relate to retirement. We developed the following paradigm as way to think about retirement and, indeed, life in general. We feel that there are three important dimensions in every life that deserve reflective thought and analysis: *Responsibilities, Relationships,* and *Recreation.*

- *Responsibilities* include what we perceive as our various duties, tasks, and obligations. For most of us, while working, the primary component in this category is our job. In retirement, many other day-to-day tasks of living will continue as responsibilities. Retirement also offers an opportunity to devote more time to areas we feel passionate about, or to take on new or different commitments that have the potential to give our lives fresh meaning.

227

- *Relationships* include the satisfaction we get from interacting with those around us. This encompasses the full continuum of interpersonal relationships, including spouse or partner, children, family, close and intimate friendships, casual relationships, and membership in social groups.

- *Recreation* includes all those non-work activities that give us pleasure. Hobbies, sports, and entertainment fit into this category.

We are not arguing that everyone should divide his or her life among these dimensions in equal thirds. The relative role played by each dimension will vary from person to person, and indeed, may vary for a particular individual at different times throughout his or her life. What we do believe is important, however, is to think through each of these dimensions of your life in terms of how important that dimension is to you, and how much energy and time should be devoted to it. We believe that it is highly unlikely that any individual will find satisfaction without paying at least some significant attention to each of these three dimensions. No one formula fits all, so everyone should think through their own personal weighting of these dimensions to achieve a life that is satisfying for them.

Retirement provides both the necessity and opportunity to readjust these components of our lives. Many people about to enter retirement feel these three components have been out of balance, because work responsibilities have dominated their lives. We have spoken to many people who complained that work obligations took so much of their time that they had little time or energy left for family or for recreation. One person felt that for years there had been no time for recreation, so when he retired he intended to spend all his time fishing. He soon found that this was not satisfying to him. He felt a vague sense of uselessness and dissatisfaction at no longer having any area of responsibility in which he was meeting challenges and making a significant contribution.

Many people respond to retirement in this way. When retirement comes they over-react and think they will be happy having no work responsibilities at all, and moving the responsibilities component of their lives to zero. Using the Three R's paradigm, such people might more easily see that having some responsibilities in their lives might be necessary for them to feel fully satisfied. They might be happier finding some other activity, for fewer hours per week, but still something that they feel makes a contribution and gives their lives a sense of purpose and meaning. The Three R's paradigm puts this into a broader perspective that makes it easier to think about one's needs and how they might be addressed.

Responsibilities need not be a burden. Indeed, they may be things that give direction and meaning to our lives. It would be a great mistake to think responsibilities end with retirement. Many of the day-to-day responsibilities of living will certainly continue. Other outlets for this "R" can be found in new ways when we are not driven by the need to earn a daily living, and not constrained to think of responsibilities only in terms of our job. However, to ignore this entire dimension of life would, for many, be a mistake.

Another thing that sometimes happens when one or both members of a couple are retiring is that the dynamics of the relationship change. We know one woman whose husband retired while she was still busy, active, and involved in numerous projects. She found herself frustrated at what she described as him "following me around all day." She resisted this level of exposure because it was not part of their former relationship pattern. Neither of them had anticipated that his free time would disrupt a life pattern that was very satisfactory to her. If they had openly discussed the Three R's before he retired, they might have realized that these patterns would change. The Three R's could give them a useful framework to think about and discuss these important issues.

Another mistake that people make is to assume that one of these dimensions will just "take care of itself." One person expected to spend a lot more time with her grandchildren. She discovered that things just didn't work out as smoothly as she had naively expected that they would. The children were extremely busy and less receptive to visits than she had hoped. She also discovered that the time spent with her grandchildren was not as satisfying as she had expected. Because she entered retirement with only a vague set of expectations, she found herself disappointed.

People about to enter retirement would benefit from thinking about the three dimensions of Responsibilities, Relationships, and Recreation. Retirement offers a wonderful opportunity to rebalance these dimensions of our lives to make them more satisfying.

The Myth of Found Time

One of the things that many people look forward to in retirement is finding more time. They assume that when they remove the huge time commitment that is connected to their work life, there will be lots of "found time" for the things that they want to do in retirement. What has surprised us in our discussions with retirees is that, for many people, the promise of found time turns out to be a myth.

We did talk to some people who found that they had a great deal of free time when they retired. Some of them even found themselves a bit at loose ends when they retired, and reported that the things they had looked forward to doing when they were retired were enjoyable, but not enough to fill their lives. They were floundering a bit, looking for things to do, seeking ways to put meaningful activity into their lives.

But such people, in our experience, were in the minority. We have been struck by the large number of people who thought they would have lots of extra time when they retired, but discovered that this was a myth. If you are a person who isn't retired but often feels much too busy, don't expect that you will find lots of extra time after you retire. Many people we interviewed said that the thing that surprised them most in retirement was how busy they were. We often heard phrases like these:

"I'm busier now than before I retired."

"I don't know where the time goes."

"I don't know how I possibly managed to keep up with everything when I was working."

"I'm just as far behind now as I was before I retired."

"I don't know how I did all this before I retired and still had time to work."

How can it be that after taking 40-plus hours per week out of someone's schedule they can still find themselves too busy? One reason is the increasing complexity of modern life. There seem to be multiple demands on our time that we have little or no control over. There is also is what one might call the failed promise of technology. Many of the technological advances that were supposed to simplify our lives have in fact made them more complex. We may be more controlled by our cell phones, our, and our use of the internet than we realize, and all of these things can easily expand to fill any available free time. Technology was supposed to save us time, but in reality, technology has simply allowed us to do more—and we do. Most people today are living in the "Crazy Busy" syndrome described in Edward M. Hollowell's popular book of the same name. In modern life we expect to do a lot, and do more than one thing at a time. We drive to work, while eating breakfast, while listening to the news, while giving our friend some advice about his home repair project. Multi-tasking is the way of modern life. There is no reason to believe that any of this will change just because you are retired. All of these pressures will still be present in your life after retirement.

There also is a tendency for tasks to expand to fill the time available. Take, for example, e-mail, internet searches, reading, or watching television. All of these are highly engaging (with entire industries behind them trying to figure out how to capture and hold our attention) and we could spend hours on any one of them. All of us can relate to the feeling of "where did the last three hours go?" The task we thought would only take 30 minutes, and might have actually have taken 30 minutes if we had a meeting with our boss coming up, now just captured the entire afternoon. This, also, is unlikely to change just because we stop working. In fact it could easily become worse, because we feel we have more time available, and there is no forced structure imposed by a work day.

What are the implications of all this as you plan for retirement?

- Don't expect that you will automatically find lots of free time after you retire. If you have a big "To Do" list now, and often find yourself saying you don't have enough time to do all the things you want to do, you'll probably be saying the same thing in retirement. Although it may seem logical that taking forty or more hours or more of work-related activity out of your life should lead to lots of free time, it simply doesn't seem to work that way. If you're finding yourself now saying, "I don't know where the time goes," there's a fairly good chance you'll be saying the same thing after you retire. The myth is that there will be lots of found time. The reality is that many people discover the extra hours have evaporated, and don't even know where the time went.

- The need for discipline, planning, and prioritizing won't go away after retirement. In fact, in some ways the need for discipline is greater after retirement than it was before. While a person is still working, there usually is a great deal of structure and required discipline built in to every working day. After retirement, when our days are less structured, it is easy to discover that time just slips away. We know retirees who, without the structure of work, often found themselves padding around in their pajamas when lunchtime arrived, wondering what they had done all morning. Don't assume that without doing something pro-active to organize your time, you will be able to do all those things you've been saying you'll do when you retire. Setting priorities, planning your time, and disciplining yourself to do the most important tasks first, will remain as important in retirement as they always were.

- Keep a careful watch on new demands on your time that may emerge after you retire. Retirees often experience many new demands on their time, as others hear that they are retired and they get numerous requests to do volunteer work, to help out at the church or synagogue or with other local organizations, to become involved in various causes, or to help care for grandchildren. If you want to discover the free time in retirement that you hoped for, you may have to build in periods of uncommitted time, and keep a firm grip on your response to the constant barrage of incoming demands. If you don't choose your new commitments wisely, there may be a kind of "commitment creep" that will end up with you feeling just as overly busy as you were before you retired. You need to think of time as a resource to be cultivated and controlled. If you don't actively manage your time, you are likely to find that it has disappeared.

The transition to retirement poses an interesting dilemma when it comes to time. Some retirees say the thing they look forward to most in retirement is not being controlled by a daily schedule forced on them by their work. One retiree told us, for example, that what she looked forward to in retirement was not having to get up with the alarm clock every morning and begin her workday routine. On the other hand, unless you impose some structure, you may find that the hours, days, and weeks have just slipped away, and you haven't done the things you wanted to do. It will be a continuing challenge to balance the desire for freedom and flexibility with the need for some structure and discipline.

One of the primary reasons people retire is to have more time. It is critical to understand that this may not happen automatically. The issue of finding time for the important activities of our lives is one that requires thought, reflection, discipline, and control over some very compelling forces that often conspire to pull time away from us. Using time well is always important, and always hard.

How Important Is Planning?

When we first started this project we felt very strongly that planning for retirement was important. We felt there was a very strong case to be made that planning for retirement would make it satisfactory and that those who didn't plan had a far greater chance of finding themselves bored and disillusioned with retirement. We no longer feel that it's quite that simple.

The case for planning can seem compelling. "We plan our careers," said retirement expert Dr. Phyllis Moen, "But we don't plan our retirement. And yet retirement may last 20 or 30 years, longer for some people than their work years. We need to see retirement as a passage to a new opportunity."[3] Ruth Cohen, a Beaverton, Oregon geriatric specialist, states: "For the first time in history, older people have a plethora of choices. But unless you have a plan, you're not likely to get what you want."[4] Even the old adage attributed to Fred Astaire: "Old age is like everything else, to make the most of it you've got to start young" is part of the folk wisdom in this area.

We have come to think that this view is oversimplified. Instead of focusing on the idea that everyone needs to have a detailed plan, we should be focusing on differences in *people*, *personal styles*, and *situations*. While there can be little doubt that for many people having clear goals and detailed plans can be useful, many others do not operate that way. Many retirement situations simply don't allow for that kind of planning. For some people having a plan is essential—for others less so. For some people their retirement will allow time for a plan, for others retirement may be unexpected, or driven by external circumstances. A one-size-fits-all model for retirement planning does not work.

We need to begin by realizing that the word "planning" can encompass a very wide range of possibilities. Even the personal definition of the word "planning" can vary widely. Consider what it means to plan for a trip. For some people it means detailed lists, notes, internet research, budget analysis, priority lists, and check-off lists of items to bring, places to go and things to do. For others, it means only that we agree on a time and a destination, and work out everything else as we go along. Because the word "planning" means such different things to different people, the overly simplistic conclusion that "planning is important" becomes almost meaningless.

When it comes to retirement, "planning" can encompass a broad range of process steps. It begins when we hear others talk about retirement, and wonder what retirement might look like for us. We start to form images of what our own retirement might be like, and these images can become even more specific, in a kind of "mental rehearsal." For some of us, the planning becomes more concrete as we articulate our thoughts to others. By talking about our plans and putting them into

236

words they become more and more tangible. For many of us this will be the full extent of our planning. Others of us will go farther, preparing a written statement of our goals, options, opportunities and perhaps even a detailed step by step outline. All of these different things might be described as "planning" for retirement.

Additionally, different people have very different personal styles. Forcing someone into a paradigm that is not in their style seems counterproductive. Situations also vary. Some people will have a long advanced time to consider their retirement possibilities, but the victim of a serious medical event, or a job downsizing, will not. For people like this, the only option for planning will be to plan after their retirement begins. The six people profiled in this book help us see the wide range of possibilities concerning planning.

Of the people profiled in this book, most of the retirements were driven by external circumstances. Jimmy Carter got fired, Bessie Delany retired to take care of her ailing mother, Katharine Hepburn retired to care for Spencer Tracy, and Arthur Ashe retired from tennis due to health problems. Carter and Ashe did lots of planning and careful thinking *after* their retirement about what would bring them satisfaction. Both Carter and Ashe were equipped with a high level of personal insight, personal awareness, and thoughtful reflection about what would bring them satisfaction. In contrast, Lee Iacocca had plenty of time to plan a satisfactory retirement, but he entered retirement with a vague and imprecise plan. His stated retirement goals showed a lack of insight about what would truly bring him personal satisfaction. Iacocca had spent his life attending to the needs and demands of the corporate world, and seemed less in touch with his own needs, and less able to establish realistic goals and plans that would bring him happiness.

Planning is a nice idea, but everyone profiled in this book had to actively re-invent their retirement as they moved through it. In fact most of their retirements were driven by external circumstances. Planning was an ongoing process in continuing need of revision. Most of the people in this book were successful in retirement because they continually weighed, re-evaluated and re-adjusted their goals as the situations required.

So what final conclusions can we come to about planning? It is important for people entering retirement to identify meaningful and realistic goals for themselves. It is critical to know yourself. Knowing yourself means knowing what kinds of goals will be meaningful to you *personally*. In considering the role of planning and establishing goals in a successful retirement, here are some ideas to keep in mind. Your retirement is likely to be more satisfactory if you:

- **Establish personally meaningful goals**. The person we described above who retired to go fishing discovered that fishing was fine as a hobby, but not rewarding enough to fill his life. It's important to evaluate what is going to be meaningful to you personally. For some fishing would be enough, for others it would not.

- **Set goals that are realistic**. Look honestly at your own past to see what works for you, and what is likely to work in retirement. We know people who moved from the Northeast to Florida, only to discover that they missed their friends and community, and soon moved back north. Others said they were going to write books when they retired, although they had never written anything before. None of them ever did write a book. It is nice to be ambitious, but not at the expense of being realistic. We are happiest when we set goals that we have a realistic chance of accomplishing. In planning your retirement goals, take into account an honest assessment of your abilities and your level of motivation.

- **Don't expect that retirement will take care of itself.** If you just drift into retirement, you may find yourself far less satisfied. You face the danger that you have made some implicit assumptions based more on the larger culture instead of your personal evaluation of what will work for you. How often have you heard the clichéd retirement advice that you don't need to think about when to retire, "You'll just know when it's time." It seems to us this is an excuse used as a substitute for thoughtful reflection.

- **Try not to change too many things all at once**. Smaller incremental changes often work better. If a new direction is required, think about ways to keep consistency in some areas of your life. Change can be more challenging than you expect, and it can be helpful to have some areas of your life that remain stable.

- **Try to be flexible and re-evaluate your goals and plans as you go along.** A plan doesn't have to be forever. Circumstances will change, goals and desires will change, and you should expect that some of your plans will not work out as you had hoped. Re-adjusting goals and rethinking plans is part of the process.

- **Don't expect perfection.** Expect to have second thoughts. Nothing is perfect, and retirement won't be either. The idea of "an endless summer" sounds much better in anticipation than it turns out to be in reality.

- **Try to retire *to* something rather than *from* something.** Those who think of retirement as simply ending their work lives are usually less satisfied than those who find enthusiasm for new projects and possibilities. Retirement should be something to look forward to, not just because one chapter of your life is ending, but because a new chapter is beginning. It is hard to be positive if you focus only on what you have left behind, or why you are leaving. By focusing on what lies ahead you can develop a much more optimistic and enthusiastic point of view.

- **Develop your own retirement "story."** It is important to be able to put into words what you plan on doing in retirement, both for those who ask, and for yourself. One indication that you have a clear picture of your retirement goals is the ability to express that in words to someone else. This means more than saying "I'm now going to have time to enjoy life." We are talking here about a narrative with specific information about what you intend to do.

Talk and Communication Matters

The language people use to describe a thing has powerful and pervasive effects. It has an impact not only on others, but more importantly, on ourselves. As we use a certain language to describe our retirement to others, we actively create the meaning of retirement for ourselves. Language gives a significant shape to an idea. This is especially true of the concept of retirement. Everyone we have interviewed or talked to has said they do not like the word "retirement." The word retirement implies stopping or ending something—it focuses on what we will be leaving behind. We need instead to be focusing on what we *will* be doing. We need a language that articulates the positive transition to a new and satisfying stage of life. It is important to be able to put into words how we conceive this next stage of our lives. The very act of using positive language helps us perceive this transition in a more positive light.

The profiles in this book illustrate the idea that language gives shape to our perception. Lee Iacocca used a negative language for his retirement, drawn from the old vocabulary of the industrial age. He viewed the world of work as a man's macho world of competition and drive, of takeovers and downsizing, of the players and the vanquished. This led to a language of "either-or." Either you are "in" or you are "out." Either you are "working," or you are "done" and "finished" and the significant work of your life is "over." In the old industrial language of retirement, you worked until you were "worn out" and then you "stopped."

When Iacocca was asked about retirement while he was at Chrysler, he said: "After 46 years in the mines? It's going to be traumatic!" And it was. Iacocca had no expectation, and

241

thus no language, to describe another stage of exciting and productive life, different from his work years. Iacocca had only the old notion of retirement, instead of the more positive concept of a productive transition to new and exciting things. For Iacocca, work was *the* thing, in his eyes, that gave meaning to life. If there was any transition for Iacocca it was only a transition to a kind of blank and empty space, because the central thing that had given meaning to his life had ended. For Iacocca there was not a language of, nor reality of, redefinition or transformation.

It is unfortunate that this creative and energetic person did not have a language that would have helped create and shape some of the exciting possibilities that were open to him. This stage of his life was not really about "quitting." It was about a major life transformation that could have been very positive. But nothing in his language reflected that.

In contrast, Ashe, Carter, and Hepburn had far more positive ways to describe their transitions to retirement. For Ashe, even when facing the grimmest possibilities of his own decline and death, he always described things in positive and constructive ways. We feel his language had a value—even to him. Speaking in these constructive terms literally created a reality that allowed him to transcend even the most disadvantaged situation. Ashe's language was never the language of blame, criticism, or condemnation. It was a language of hope, beauty and gratitude. We feel that his language and his positive way of looking at his situation allowed him to live his life fully and productively right to the end.

Like Ashe, Carter also used positive language in the face of an extremely challenging and difficult situation. Carter refused to fall into a pattern of blame and retribution. He always seemed to use his language to describe his circumstances in ways that created a new and more positive reality. Possibly his religious convictions and his years in political life contributed to his ability to be transformative with language.

Similarly, Hepburn always talked about her dedication to Tracy in the most positive and glowing terms. Hard as it was to believe, she described her time caring for Tracy as some of the best years of her life. And every account seems to support the conclusion that this is honestly how she saw it. She always saw the glass half-full instead of half-empty. There never was even a hint of negative talk or self pity.

In every one of the examples above the language the person used was integrally related to their constructive outlook. In part, their language *arose from* their positive attitude, but it part their language *helped to form* their positive outlook.

What we can learn from this is that we need to find different ways to talk about retirement that do not carry negative images of termination and loss. The word retirement in our culture often carries powerful negative overtones. In contemplating our own retirement it would be far better to describe it as a constructive transition to a new stage of our lives, a stage that can be exciting, productive and fulfilling. We all make a choice by the words we use to describe something. It is our belief that more positive language has the potential to lead to a more positive conception of retirement itself. As each of us constructs our own narrative of our transition to retirement, we need to find our own uniquely positive language to describe it.

Attitude and Happiness

One of the most striking things about the people we have profiled in this book is how many of them had such positive attitudes. The Delany sisters offered a wonderful model of retaining a positive attitude when confronted with obstacles and adversity, even in the face of pervasive racism and social prejudice. This positive approach stayed with them throughout their lives and made their retirement rich and rewarding. Katharine Hepburn kept her enthusiasm and energetic approach to life even while coping with the decline and death of her life-long partner. Arthur Ashe retained his positive outlook in the face of his health problems, the early demise of a brilliant athletic career, and his terminal battle with AIDS. Jimmy Carter converted his unexpected loss of power and prestige into the most successful post presidential "retirement" in history, largely through the power of his positive, determined, and constructive outlook. There is a strong message here for all of us. Having a positive attitude may be the single most important factor in making our retirement all that it can be.

Positive attitudes, such as those mentioned above, may come in part from personality characteristics we are born with. However, research described earlier in this book suggests optimism can be learned, and our attitudes are largely under our control. Our self-talk has a powerful influence on how we frame things and how we respond to them. To a considerable extent, our reactions derive from our attitudes, and our attitudes derive from the things we tell ourselves.

If some aspects of our retirement initially strike us as losses, we can push ourselves to look at things differently. We can reframe the situation. We can talk to ourselves in a different way. We can explicitly make comparisons to others who have less than we do, and remind ourselves of our blessings. If some of our relationships are lost, we can focus on relationships that still exist. If some of our previous life patterns are forced to change, we can focus on our new opportunities, and positive memories. If physical limitations begin to constrain us, we can discover ways to get enjoyment from our daily lives despite those limitations.

For some, such re-framing comes naturally out of our past experiences. For others, we may make an explicit decision to revise our self-talk because we realize that our talk helps form our reality. In our experience, and based on the profiles in this book, those with the most satisfying retirements found positive ways to talk about this stage of their lives, even when faced with severe challenges.

For many in today's society, the retirement years will be longer and filled with more potential than ever before in history. If we enter this period thoughtfully, retirement can truly be the beginning of the most fulfilling and rewarding years of our lives.

LIFE AFTER WORK

For Further Reading

In writing this book we found valuable information in several other works. All of them are fascinating and filled with interesting material. We hope that reading this book will encourage you to read these other works as well. We have cited what we have used, but it represents only a tiny portion of the wealth of interesting information in these fine works. We recommend that you read the original works. All of them are extremely good reads and reveal subtle and interesting details that are not part of the general public knowledge of these fascinating people. Listed below are a few of the works we think you will enjoy.

The Delany Sisters:

Having Our Say: the Delany Sisters' First 100 Years, by Sarah Louise and Annie Elizabeth Delany, with Amy Hill Hearth, published by Kodansha America, Inc., 1993.

On My Own at 107: Reflections on Life Without Bessie, by Sarah L. Delany with Amy Hill Hearth, published by Harper Collins, 1997.

Lee Iacocca:

Iacocca: An Autobiography, by Lee Iacocca with William Novak, published by Bantam Books, Inc., 1984.

Talking Straight, by Lee Iacocca, published by Bantam Books, 1988.

Katharine Hepburn:

An Affair to Remember by Christopher Andersen, published by William Morrow and Company, 1997.

Me, by Katharine Hepburn, published by Alfred Knopf, 1991.

Jimmy Carter:

The Virtues of Aging, by Jimmy Carter, published by Ballantine Publishing Group, 1998.

Everything to Gain: Making the Most of the Rest of Your Life, by Jimmy Carter and Rosalynn Carter, published by Random House, 1987.

Arthur Ashe:

Days of Grace, by Arthur Ashe with Arnold Rampersad, published by Ballantine Books, 1994.

LIFE AFTER WORK

Notes

Chapter 1 - The Promise of Retirement

[1] Joel S. Savishinsky, *Breaking the Watch: The Meanings of Retirement in America* (Ithaca, NY: Cornell University Press, 2000).

Chapter 2 - The Delany Sisters: Living Long

[1] Terri Needels and Toby Lilanow, "Power Up Your Brain," *Psychology Today*, August 2002, p. 44.

[2] Although the average life expectancy today at birth is 76.7 years, the life expectancy of someone who has already survived to age 55 is longer. In 1998 the average 55 year old could expect to live to age 80.5 (in 1997 that was 80.4; 78.5 for males and 82.5 for females).

[3] Sarah L. and A. Elizabeth Delany with Amy Hill Hearth, *Having Our Say: The Delany Sisters' First 100 Years* (New York: Kodansha America, 1994), p. 179.

[4] Ibid., p. 6.

[5] Ibid.

[6] Ibid., p. 7.

[7] Ibid.

[8] Ibid.

[9] Ibid., p. 12.

[10] Ibid., p. 63.

[11] Amy Hill Hearth, "Bessie and Sadie: The Delany Sisters Relive a Century," *Smithsonian* 24 (October 1993): pp. 144-162.

[12] Delany and Delany with Hearth, *Having Our Say*, p. 79.

[13] Ibid., p. 72.

[14] Ibid., p. 93.

[15] Ibid., p. 74.

[16] Ibid., p. 99.

[17] Ibid., p. 115.

[18] He lived from 1858-1928 according to the family tree in *Having Our Say*, so he was either 69 or 70.

[19] Delany and Delany with Hearth, *Having Our Say*, p. 159.

[20] In another source, it says first black woman, but in *Having our Say* (p. xii) it is clear that she was the first black person.

[21] Ibid., p. 176.

[22] Ibid., p. 177.

[23] Ibid., p. 181.

[24] Ibid., p. 183.

[25] Ibid., p. 187.

[26] Ibid., p. 194.

[27] Ibid., p. 144.

[28] Ibid., pp. 202-203.

[29] Hearth, "Bessie and Sadie: The Delany Sisters Relive a Century."

[30] Sarah L. Delany with Amy Hill Hearth, *On My Own at 107: Reflections on Life Without Bessie* (San Francisco: Harper Collins, 1997) p. xvi.

[31] Ibid.

[32] Michael Brickey, *Defy Aging* (Chapter one "You are going to live longer—Will you choose to Live Well?") www.galaxymall.com/books/drbrickey/chapter1.html.

[33] Sarah L. and A. Elizabeth Delany with Amy Hill Hearth, *The Delany Sisters' Book of Everyday Wisdom*, (New York: Kodansha America, 1994, International edition 1996), p. 33.

[34] Ibid., p. 11.

[35] David G. Myers, *The Pursuit of Happiness: Who is Happy - and Why* (New York: Avon Books, 1992).

[36] Sarah L. and A. Elizabeth Delany with Amy Hill Hearth, *The Delany Sisters' Book of Everyday Wisdom*, p. 62.

[37] Ibid., pp. 32-33.

[38] For a description and citation of numerous studies showing a relationship between happiness and religion, see Myers, *The Pursuit of Happiness*, p. 183.

[39] Martin E.P. Seligman, *Authentic Happiness: Using the New Positive Psychology to realize your Potential for Lasting Fulfillment* (New York: Free Press, 2002), p. 59.

[40] Although numerous surveys have shown that people who report being more religious also describe themselves as happier and more satisfied with life, it is not clear what causes this relationship. For a description of some of this research, and a thoughtful discussion of many possible factors that might lie behind the associations between religion and happiness, see David Myers, *The Pursuit of Happiness*, p. 183-204, and

Martin Seligman, *Authentic Happiness*, p. 59-60. Beyond the factors they discuss, we also should remember that all of this research is based on self-report, so it is possible that part of the relationship arises from religious people being more likely to describe themselves as satisfied with life because they believe they *should* be satisfied with life.

[41] Sarah L. and A. Elizabeth Delany with Amy Hill Hearth, *The Delany Sisters' Book of Everyday Wisdom*, p. 78.

[42] Ibid., p. 32-33.

[43] Martin E. P. Seligman, *Learned Optimism: How to Change Your Mind and Your Life* (New York: Simon and Schuster, 1998).

[44] Timothy Miller, *How to Want What You Have: Discovering the Magic and Grandeur of Ordinary Existence* (New York: Henry Holt, 1994).

———

Chapter 3 - Lee Iacocca: Money Isn't Enough

[1] For a fuller discussion of the research that supports this statement, see David G. Myers, *The Pursuit of Happiness: Who is Happy - and Why* (New York: Avon Books, 1992).

[2] Lee Iacocca with William Novak, *Iacocca: an Autobiography* (New York: Bantam Books paperback edition, 1986), p. 7.

[3] Ibid., p. 9.

[4] Ibid., p. 37.

[5] Ibid., p. 43.

[6] Ibid., p. 101.

[7] Ibid., p. 97.

[8] Ibid., pp. 98-99.

[9] Ibid., p. 93.

[10] Ibid., p. 155.

[11] Ibid., p. 100.

[12] Ibid., p. 100.

[13] Ibid., p. 288.

[14] Ibid., p. 123.

[15] Ibid., p. 117.

[16] Ibid., p. 301.

[17] Ibid., p. 131.

[18] Ibid., p. 127.

[19] Ibid., p. 155.

[20] Ibid., p. xv.

21 Ibid., pp. 104-105.

22 Ibid., pp. 113-114.

23 Ibid., p. 145.

24 Ibid., pp. xv-xvi.

25 Ibid., p. xi.

26 "Iacocca, Lee" Britannica Online, <www.eb.com:180/cgi-bin/g?DocF= micro/285/27.Html>[Accessed December 12, 1997].

27 www.geocities.com/SoHo/8483/iacocca.html.

28 Iacocca with Novak, p. 225.

29 Ibid p. 261.

30 Ibid p. 162.

31 "Iacocca, Lee" Britannica Online, <www.eb.com:180/cgi-bin g?DocF= micro/285/27.html.

32 http://web.lexis-nexis.com/univers/docu.

33 "Iacocca, Lee" Britannica Online, <www.eb.com:180/cgi-bin/g?DocF= micro/285/27.html.

34 Alex Taylor III, "How I Flunked Retirement," *Fortune Magazine*, June 24, 1996, p. 50.

35 Ibid.

36 Iacocca with Novak, p. xvi.

37 Ibid., p. 188.

38 Ibid., p. 188.

39 Ibid., p. 188.

40 Lee Iacocca, *Talking Straight* (New York: Bantam Books, 1988).

41 "Lee's Parting Shots" *Fortune Magazine*, September 7, 1992.

42 Ibid.

43 Ibid.

44 Ibid.

45 Ibid.

46 Ibid.

47 Taylor, "How I Flunked Retirement," p. 50.

48 Ibid.

49 Ibid.

50 Mark Phelan, "Look Who's Talking: Lee Iacocca." Interview reported in AI-online, April 1998. :www.ai-online.com/articles/4talk.htm.

51 Taylor, "How I Flunked Retirement," p. 50.

52 Ibid.

53 Ibid.

54 Ibid.

[55] Ibid.

[56] Ibid.

[57] Phelan, "Look Who's Talking: Lee Iacocca."

[58] *Time* magazine, February 1, 1999.

[59] Ibid.

[60] David G. Myers, *The Pursuit of Happiness: Who is Happy - and Why* (New York: Avon Books, 1992).

[61] Ibid., p. 44.

[62] Martin E.P. Seligman, *Authentic Happiness: Using the New Positive Psychology to realize your Potential for Lasting Fulfillment* (New York: Free Press, 2002).

[63] "Lee's Parting Shots" *Fortune Magazine*, September 7, 1992.

[64] Bob Buford, *Halftime: Changing Your Game Plan from Success to Significance* (Grand Rapids, MI: Zondervan Publishing House, 1994).

[65] Taylor, "How I Flunked Retirement," p. 50.

[66] Iacocca with Novak, p. 50.

[67] Ibid.

[68] Ibid., p. 63.

Chapter 4 - Katharine Hepburn: Taking Care

[1] Frederic M. Hudson, *The Adult Years: Mastering the Art of Self-Renewal* (San Francisco: Jossey-Bass, revised edition, 1999), pp. 130-131.

[2] Caroline Latham, *Katharine Hepburn*, (New York: Chelsea House, 1988), p. 23.

[3] Ibid., p. 21.

[4] There is considerable confusion about Katharine Hepburn's age because she reported her birth date differently at different times. For many years she said her birthday was November 8, but that was actually her brother's birthday, not her own. She adopted Tom's birthday as her own, and also claimed the year of her birth to be two years later than it actually was.

[5] Ibid.

[6] Christopher Andersen, *An Affair To Remember*, (New York: William Morrow and Company, 1997), p. 36.

[7] Ibid., p. 37.

[8] Latham, p. 24.

[9] Ibid., p. 50.

[10] Ibid., p. 47.

[11] Ibid., p. 51.
[12] Ibid., p. 57.
[13] Ibid., p. 112.
[14] Ibid., p. 111.
[15] Ibid., p. 112.
[16] Ibid., p. 167.
[17] Ibid., p. 125.
[18] Ibid., p. 122.
[19] Ibid., p. 124.
[20] Ibid., p. 132.
[21] Ibid., p. 132.
[22] Ibid., p. 148.
[23] Ibid., p. 112.
[24] Ibid., p. 181.
[25] Ibid., p. 230.
[26] Ibid., p. 140.
[27] Ibid., p. 73.
[28] Ibid., p. 100.
[29] Ibid., p. 100.
[30] Ibid., p. 138.
[31] Ibid., p. 100.
[32] Ibid., p. 101.
[33] Ibid., p. 90.
[34] Ibid., Loretta Young (pp. 81-82), Myrna Loy (pp. 85-86), Joan Crawford (p. 98), Ingrid Bergman (p. 105).
[35] Ibid., p. 162.
[36] Ibid., p. 73.
[37] Ibid., p. 101.
[38] Ibid., p. 149.
[39] Ibid., p. 149.
[40] Ibid., p. 164.
[41] Ibid., p. 151.
[42] Ibid., p. 150.
[43] Ibid., p. 164.
[44] Ibid., p. 163.
[45] Latham, p. 178.
[46] Ibid., p. 181.
[47] Andersen, p 235.
[48] Ibid., p. 239.

[49] Ibid.

[50] Ibid, p. 251.

[51] Katharine Hepburn, *Me* (New York: Alfred Knopf, 1991), pp. 389-395.

[52] Ibid., pp. 399-400.

[53] Andersen, pp. 224-230, p. 245.

[54] Barbara Leaming, **Katharine Hepburn** (New York: Crown Publishers, 1995) p. 480.

[55] Andersen, p. 265.

[56] Latham, p. 19.

[57] Ibid., p. 85.

[58] We put the work "retired" in quotes because in some ways this was a retirement but in other ways it was simply a work stoppage to help her mate. But at this time in her career it could be assumed a work stoppage would most likely result in the practical end to Katharine Hepburn's career. Also it is important to remember that Tracy's condition might have continued much longer than the five years it did. In every way it was a courageous choice.

[59] Latham, p. 63.

[60] Ibid., p. 85.

[61] Ibid., p. 86.

[62] Ibid., p. 87.

[63] Andersen, p. 297.

[64] Ibid.

[65] Ibid., pp. 3-8. This account is virtually identical to that by Leaming, in **Katharine Hepburn,** 1985, pp. 493-495. Both of these accounts are drawn heavily from Katharine Hepburn's autobiography, **Me: Stories of My Life**. Gary Carey, in **Katharine Hepburn: A Hollywood Yankee,** 1983, pp. 213-214, gives a briefer and somewhat different account. Anne Edwards, in **A Remarkable Woman**, 1985 pp. 343-344, gives a brief account that agrees with Carey. The two earlier accounts both have Hepburn arriving after his death. More recent, and more detailed, accounts have her with him when he dies.

[66] Hepburn, p. 403.

[67] Andersen, p. 299.

[68] Gary Carey, **Katharine Hepburn: A Hollywood Yankee** (New York: St. Martin's Press, 1983), p. 214.

[69] Virginia E. Richardson, **Retirement Counseling: a Handbook for Gerontology Practitioners** (New York: Springer Publishing Company, 1993), p. 158.

[70] Ibid., 159.

[71] Joel S. Savishinsky, *Breaking the Watch: The Meanings of Retirement in America* (Ithaca, NY: Cornell University Press, 2000), p. 17. He makes reference to several sources on care giving and retirement; his references to percentages on women care givers are from Brubaker and Brubaker in 1992.

[72] Richardson, p. 159.

[73] Betty Friedan, *Fountain of Age*, (New York: Simon and Schuster, 1993), p. 149, citing research by Neugarten, 1970.

[74] Hudson, *The Adult Years: Mastering the Art of Self-Renewal.*

[75] Richardson p. 159. Richardson cites research by Brody in 1990 and Hayes & Deren 1990 to support these conclusions.

[76] Friedan, p. 150.

[77] Ibid.

[78] Ibid.

[79] Ibid., p, 197.

[80] Ibid., p, 149.

[81] Ibid.

[82] Ibid.

———

Chapter 5 - Jimmy Carter: Reinventing a Life

[1] Dory Hollander, *The Doom Loop System*, (New York: Viking Penguin, 1991), p. 182.

[2] Ibid., p. 183.

[3] Ibid., p. 184.

[4] Bob Buford, *Half Time: Changing Your Game Plan from Success to Significance* (Grand Rapids Michigan: Zondervan Publishing House, 1994).

[5] Douglas Brinkley, *The Unfinished Presidency: Jimmy Carter's Journey Beyond the White House*, (New York: Viking Press, 1998), p. 2.

[6] Gary Smith, "What makes Jimmy run?", *Life Magazine,* November, 1995 http://www.life.com/Life/essay/carter/carter07.html.

[7] Jimmy Carter, *The Virtues of Aging* (New York: The Ballantine Publishing Group, 1998), p. 1.

[8] Ibid., p. 3.

[9] Hollander, p. 205.

[10] Carter, p. 2.

[11] Jimmy Carter and Rosalynn Carter, *Everything to Gain: Making the Most of the Rest of Your Life* (New York: Random House, 1987), p. 23.

[12] Ibid.

[13] Ibid., p. 27.

[14] Ibid., p. 28.

[15] Carter, p. 4.

[16] Interview by Tracy Thompson, *The Washington Post*, "Action Aging: Jimmy and Rosalynn Carter Find Retirement Liberating," Sunday, October 25 1998.

[17] Ibid.

[18] Ibid.

[19] Ibid.

[20] Interview by Mary Bridgman: "Involvement, Purpose Key to Carter's Happy Aging," in *The Columbus Dispatch*, October 28, 1998.

[21] Brinkley, p. xvi-xvii.

[22] Ibid., p. xv.

[23] Carter and Carter, p. 31.

[24] The Carter Center Brochure (undated).

[25] Carter and Carter, p. 33.

[26] Carter said "it was incredibly frustrating watching Reagan's people undermine so much of my agenda." (Brinkley, p. 57). Reagan's administration permitted the environmentally unconscionable sale of oil and gas leases on eighty-one tracts off the coast of California. For a fuller explanation of the programs that were dismantled, see Brinkley, pp.. 57-58. Brinkley lists more than 18 changes made by the Reagan administration.

[27] Brinkley, p. xix.

[28] Address by Gunnar Berge, Chairman of the Norwegian Nobel Committee, Oslo, December 10, 2002.

[29] Smith, "What makes Jimmy run?"

[30] Carter and Carter, p. 189.

[31] Interview by Elizabeth Kurylo, in *The Atlanta Journal and Constitution* March 22, 1997, p. A02.

[32] Interview by Mary Bridgman, "Involvement, Purpose Key to Carter's Happy Aging," in *The Columbus Dispatch*, October 28, 1998.

[33] Smith, "What makes Jimmy run?"

[34] David G. Myers, *The Pursuit of Happiness: Who is Happy - and Why* (New York: Avon Books, 1992).

[35] Carter and Carter, p. 190.

[36] *Business Week*, July 20 1998, Commentary by Jimmy Carter pp. 112-113.

[37] Carter and Carter, p. 189.

[38] Ibid, p. 191.

Chapter 6 - Arthur Ashe: Coping With Adversity

[1] Ted Weissberg, *Arthur Ashe* (New York: Chelsea House, 1991), p. 26.

[2] Arthur Ashe and Neil Amdur, *Arthur Ashe: Off The Court* (New York: New American Library, 1981), pp. 19-20. *Days of Grace* has a slightly different version of this story.

[3] Arthur Ashe with Arnold Rampersad, *Days of Grace* (New York: Ballantine Books, 1994), p. 4.

[4] Based on statements Ashe makes in *Days of Grace*, pp. 3-4.

[5] Ibid., p. 42.

[6] Ibid., p. 58.

[7] Bob Carter, "Ashe's Impact Reached Far Beyond the Court." retrieved 1-27-06 from http://espn.go.com/classic/biography/s/Ashe_Arthur.html.

[8] Ashe with Rampersad, p. 3.

[9] Ibid pp. 41-42.

[10] Caroline Lazo, *Arthur Ashe*, A & E Biography series, (Minneapolis, MN: Lerner Publications Company, 1999), pp. 52-53. Also see Ashe and Amdur, p. 69.

[11] Lazo, p. 48, and Ashe and Amdur, pp. 53-54.

[12] Ashe with Rampersad, p. 36.

[13] Ibid., p. 38.

[14] Ibid., pp. 38-39.

[15] Ibid., p. 39.

[16] Ibid., p. 41.

[17] Ibid., p. 101.

[18] Ibid., p. 41.

[19] Ibid., p. 79.

[20] Ibid., p. 70.

[21] Ibid., p. 81.

[22] Ibid., p. 100.

[23] Ibid., p. 101.

[24] Ibid., p. 40.

[25] Ibid.

[26] Ibid., p. 48.

[27] Ibid., p. 174.

[28] Bob Carter, "Ashe's Impact Reached Far Beyond the Court." retrieved 1-27-06 from http://espn.go.com/classic/biography/s/Ashe_Arthur.html.

[29] Ashe with Rampersad, p. 17.

[30] S. L. Price, quoted in *Days of Grace* p. 31.

[31] Ashe with Rampersad, pp. 31-32.

[32] Ibid., p. 262.

[33] Mary Huzinec, Maria Speidel, Rochelle Jones, and Sarah Skolnik, "Man of Grace and Glory," *People* magazine, February 22, 1993, pp. 61-62, 68-72. Cited in Gonzales Doreen, *Aids: Ten Stories of Courage* (Springfield, NJ: Enslow Publishers, 1996), p. 94.

[34] Lazo, p. 119, quoting Frank Deford, "Lessons from a Friend," *Newsweek* magazine, February 22, 1993, p. 60.

[35] Ashe with Rampersad, p. 126.

[36] Ibid., p. 128.

[37] Ibid., p. 299.

[38] David G. Myers, *The Pursuit of Happiness: Who is Happy - and Why* (New York: Avon Books, 1992).

[39] Ashe with Rampersad, p. 297.

[40] Ibid., p. 295.

[41] Ibid., p. 278.

[42] Ibid., p. 299.

[43] Ibid., p. 303.

[44] Ibid., p. 281.

[45] Ibid., p. 285.

[46] Ibid., p. 304.

Chapter 7 Final Reflections

[1] Joel S. Savishinsky, "The Unbearable Lightness of Retirement: Ritual and Support in a Modern Life Passage." *Research on Aging*, Vol. 17, No.3, (September 1995), pp. 243-259.

[2] S. Gilbert, "New Portrait of Retiring is Emerging," *New York Times*, May 29, 2001.

[3] Ibid.

[4] Quoted in Ralph Warener, *Get a Life: You Don't need a Million to Retire Well*, (Berkley CA: Nolo Press, 4th Edition, 2002), p. 11.

LIFE AFTER WORK

Index

261

About the Authors

DR. ARTHUR F. DAURIA is Professor and Chair of the Communication Arts Department at the State University of New York at Oneonta, New York. He received his Ph.D in Communication Studies from the Pennsylvania State University. He is a recipient of the Chancellors Award for excellence in teaching, the highest teaching award for the State University of New York system. He taught at Penn State before coming to Oneonta. He teaches courses related to interpersonal communication, human interaction, and conflict management.

DR. WALTER VOM SAAL is a Professor of Psychology at the State University of New York at Oneonta, where he teaches courses in aging and in human sexuality. He received his undergraduate degree from Columbia University and his Ph.D. from McMaster University in Hamilton, Ontario. He also has served as a college academic vice president, and interim college president. He taught at Princeton University and Millersville University before coming to Oneonta, and was awarded the Commonwealth of Pennsylvania Distinguished Teaching Chair, the highest teaching award in the Pennsylvania System of Higher Education.

The authors have enjoyed working together for many years to study and explore the topic of retirement. Their research on this topic included interviews, surveys, focus groups, and workshops.